Did Ancient Chinese Explore America?

My Journey Through the Rocky Mountains to Find Answers

Charlotte Harris Rees

Torchflame Books

Copyright © 2013 by Charlotte Harris Rees

Did Ancient Chinese Explore America?
My Journey Through the Rocky Mountains to Find Answers

www.asiaticfathers.com
HarrisMaps@msn.com

Published 2013 by Torchflame Books
www.lightmessages.com
Durham, NC 27713
Printed in the United States of America
ISBN: 978-1-61153-080-3

Also by Charlotte Harris Rees:

Secret Maps of the Ancient World (2008, 2009)

Chinese Sailed to America Before Columbus: More Secrets from the Dr. Hendon M. Harris, Jr. Map Collection (2011)

Editor: *The Asiatic Fathers of America* (2006)

ALL RIGHTS RESERVED

No part of this publication may be reproduced, stored in a retrieval system, or transmitted in any form or by any means, electronic, mechanical, photocopying, recording, scanning, or otherwise, except as permitted under Section 107 or 108 of the 1976 International Copyright Act, without the prior written permission except in brief quotations embodied in critical articles and reviews.

This book is dedicated to my husband, Dave Rees, and to my brother, Hendon Harris, III

They were both wonderful companions during my adventure of following the *Shan Hai Jing* Rocky Mountain journey.

I could not have completed the trip without them.

Dave took most of the photos for this book and drew several of the enclosed maps.

Contents

Preface I
Introduction V
1 – An American Mystery 1
2 – Casper, Wyoming 8
3 – Medicine Bow Peak, Wyoming 19
4 – Longs Peak, Colorado 30
5 – Grays Peak, Colorado 38
6 – Mount Princeton, Colorado 47
7 – Blanca Peak, Colorado 54
8 – North Truchas Peak, New Mexico 63
9 – Manzano Peak, New Mexico 76
10 – Sierra Blanca, New Mexico 92
11 – Guadalupe Mountains, Texas 100
12 – Baldy Peak on Mt. Livermore, Texas 110
13 – Chinati Peak, Texas 120
14 – Conclusions 128
Addendum - Where Was the Baldy Peak Gold Mine? 132
About The Author 135
Acknowledgements 136
Endnotes 137
Bibliography 149

Preface

Secrets arise when information is withheld or clues are ignored.

Yet, for many years I, myself, ignored proofs about America's history. Some of these secrets are in strange old Asian maps, in ancient Chinese texts, in the DNA of Native Americans, and in the very mountains and boulders of North America.

This book is a result of my quest to uncover those secrets. It is a travelogue of a trip I undertook to confirm a rumored 1100 mile ancient Chinese journey along what is now known as the eastern slope of the US Rocky Mountains.

Our trip was completed in the fall of 2012. My husband, Dave, and I had two weeks of exciting new discoveries in and among the golden aspen and beautiful fall foliage of the rugged Rockies. What the ancient Chinese text from 4000 years ago said that we would see was validated. Multiple factors show that Chinese were there. Repeated occurrences of previously carbon dated yet unexplained (until now) objects along the route firmly establish the time period.

Ten years earlier I would have never dreamed of taking that journey to the Rockies with research as my motive. I was drawn (somewhat reluctantly) into this quest by a force larger than myself.

In 1972, my father, Dr. Hendon Harris, Jr., a third generation Baptist missionary, found in an antique shop in Korea an ancient Asian world map. Chinese writings indicated that they had explored a beautiful continent to their east during their first dynasty (around 2000 BC). Father recognized that continent (known in Chinese as Fu Sang) where today we place America.

After his find, Father located a few other similar maps in famous museums and collections around the world. However, at that time most regarded China, Japan, and Korea on the maps as real, but the majority of the rest of the locations as imaginary.

After much research, in 1973 Father published a book of almost 800 pages titled *The Asiatic Fathers of America* – two books in one volume: *The Chinese Discovery and Colonization of Ancient America* and *The Asiatic Kingdoms of America*. One of the sources he quoted was *Pale Ink* published in 1953 by Chicago attorney, Henriette Mertz.

Even without knowledge of maps like Father possessed, she cited numerous other proofs that early Chinese reached America.

Both my father and Mertz (who never met) based their theories on a revered text, the *Shan Hai Jing (Classic of Mountains and Seas)*, quoted down through Chinese history. However, for many years I was a skeptic of those theories. It was not anything personal against my father, it was just that the idea seemed farfetched and I was too busy with my own life to be bothered.

Father died suddenly of a stroke in January 1981. His offspring, the seven of us siblings, divided his few belongings but decided to keep his maps as a unit – just in case he was correct in his analysis. For years the maps were forgotten documents in a box under my brother's bed.

In early 2003 my husband and I had just retired with plans to travel and to take life easy when I read a book which caused me to wonder whether my father could have been right. I called my brother, Hendon, III. Shortly after that he, our spouses, and I took Father's map collection to the Library of Congress where it stayed for three years while it was studied.

Meanwhile, I begged other family members to take up our father's research about the maps. However, everyone else in the family was too busy, so the lot fell to me. Fortunately around the same time I also met professor emeritus Dr. Cyclone Covey, who has a PhD in history from Stanford University. Dr. Covey was familiar with the work of my father and that of Mertz. He had also studied the *Shan Hai Jing* for many years. Dr. Covey offered to mentor me should I decide to pick up my father's research.

Ten years later I am still delving into this subject and Dr. Covey is still my mentor. In the interim I wrote an abridgment of my father's book and now three other books. I have given presentations at many venues including the Library of Congress, the National Library of China, Stanford University, University of British Columbia, Royal Geographical Societies in London and Hong Kong, and in Switzerland, Malaysia, and across the US.

There are many academic studies that now support the thesis of early Chinese exploration in the Americas. They come from the fields of archeology, oceanography, geography and maps, biology, linguistics, art, music, and comparative religions. DNA has now linked exact Chinese and Native American families across the Pacific.

However, during my research a question continued to ring in my ears: "Was Mertz right in contending that there were exact 4000 year old Chinese trails that one could follow in the Americas?" If so, to me that was the ultimate adventure in this quest – to walk the paths of ancient Chinese explorers.

Taking the *Shan Hai Jing* and modern topographical maps, Mertz drew sketches of four separate journeys that the Chinese covered in North America. She claimed that the descriptions fit nowhere else on earth. The *Shan Hai Jing* said: "Go so far and you will see…." In each location it specified minerals, animals, and how the rivers flowed.

Early in my venture into this research, I discussed Mertz's book and the *Shan Hai Jing* with Dr. John Hebert, Chief of Geography and Maps at the Library of Congress. He suggested that I concentrate on the animals, which I did. One after another the descriptions matched up to species native only to the Americas and in the correct habitats. I wondered: "How could the Chinese know that unless they had been there?"

However, my busy speaking and writing schedule, plus the fact that I live more than half way across the North American continent from the closest of the four journeys that Mertz charted, kept me from visiting them.

The closest route to me, one that traces the Rockies, is probably the most like it was long ago. Much of that area is now national parks and nature conservancies. Some of the specified mountains are over 14,000 feet high and many wild and dangerous animals live there.

Mertz was older when she wrote her book and so had not followed those journeys in person. Apparently we were the first to follow her instruction regarding the ancient Chinese trails. By visiting the actual locations we were able to see several corollaries that even she missed.

Twice in 2009 my brother Hendon and I met in Texas to view the final stops on this *Shan Hai Jing* Rockies trip. Both times it was during the winter months when the Texas rattlesnakes were less active. We were both extremely excited about what we saw and learned there. However, years later we still had not found time to complete the rest of that journey from Wyoming going south. In fall 2012 my husband and I decided to make the trek. We kept in touch with Hendon by phone to report our progress.

After our trip I learned that archeology texts indicate that around 2000 BC an unknown group, which has been named the "McKean Complex," passed through the area that we had just visited. They are an anomaly because they were much more advanced than those before and after them. No one seems to know where they originated. However, I realized that the description of McKean Complex homes almost exactly matched dwellings of that era described in archeology books for China.

That was also the same time period which several scholars have attributed to the *Shan Hai Jing*. In that period China was one of the most advanced cultures on earth. They had carefully laid out villages. Their artisans were producing intricately painted pottery, carved jade, and silk. They had writing and domesticated animals and were cultivating vegetables while utilizing irrigation. They understood astronomy and were sea faring.

Furthermore, a map for the University of Manitoba to show the northern stretches of the McKean Complex matches another one of Mertz's *Shan Hai Jing* journeys. One can almost trace one map from the other.

I was excited to learn that in that area of the McKean Complex habitation is a large unexplained stone astronomical device with twenty eight spokes, unevenly spaced around a hub. A few years ago it was discovered that it indicates solstices and the rising of three stars. None of the Native Americans know its origin. My mind again went back to Chinese archeology texts and almost identical astronomical devices with 28 spokes unevenly spaced around a hub used in China starting in the second millennium BC.

However, these examples only scratch the surface of what is found on the North American *Shan Hai Jing* journeys – even thousands of years later. The Chinese correctly described animals native only to the Americas and correctly told about minerals and how the rivers flowed. In addition, ancient style Chinese writing and farming methods, burial and home sites positioned according to Feng Shui and Taoist principles, and unexplained plants native to China are all found in multiple locations along the route that we covered.

Recently the names of two Shang Dynasty king were discovered on petroglyphs along this route. That writing and the patina over it has been authenticated by leading experts.

Introduction

The purpose of this book is not to help one find gold or gems, though those who read it may decide to go on that treasure hunt. Neither is it to discuss my father's maps, nor to decide who arrived first in the Americas.

The purpose of this book is to determine whether the Chinese *Shan Hai Jing (Classic of the Mountains and the Seas)* is truth or fiction, and if truth, try to determine when that trip took place. If the *Shan Hai Jing* is true, it shakes the foundations of current world history texts.

The journey we took followed written instruction in the *Shan Hai Jing* which stated: "Go so far and you will see…." It should have been fairly easy to disprove.

In 1953 Henriette Mertz, a Chicago attorney, after studying topographical world maps, stated in *Pale Ink* that detailed descriptions of the Eastern journeys in the *Shan Hai Jing* fit nowhere else on earth other than North America. She charted four routes and contended that those trips took place about 2250 BC.

In 1972 Random House republished *Pale Ink*, with a few minor additions, under the new title *Gods from the Far East: How the Chinese Discovered America*.

Henriette Mertz

However, neither Mertz nor anyone else in recent times actually completed any of the journeys that she charted to see what was there. Therefore, we went.

This book is my travelogue of one of those four journeys. That trek follows the eastern slope of the Rocky Mountains from Wyoming all the way down through Texas to the Rio Grande for 1100 miles.

Along the way I briefly weave into the text some of the written history of areas we covered. The maps that we followed are Mertz's maps, not those of my father. My father's maps are part of the story, but are world maps and do not give the detail afforded by Mertz.

My basic premises:

- In 2000 an exhaustive five year study was completed to determine the start date of China's early history. That study involved hundreds of scholars from numerous disciplines. It concluded that China's first dynasty (Xia) started around 2070 BC. Therefore, in this book I do not go back earlier than that. For convenience I round it to 2000 BC.

- By 2000 BC China was an advanced culture. Western scholars such as Dr. Joseph Needham and Dr. John Hobson have verified that for most of world history China was the most advanced culture on earth.

- The *Shan Hai Jing* claims to be a survey of the entire world done at a very early date. Some believe it is the world's oldest geography.

- Some scholars contend that the *Shan Hai Jing* grew out of notes that originally accompanied maps. However, those maps have long been separated from the text.

- According to *The History of Cartography,* 72 percent of the locations shown on world maps of the ch'onhado (tian xia) style are from the *Shan Hai Jing*. My father, Dr. Hendon Harris, Jr., believed that the tian xia world maps in his collection, and the few others worldwide like them, descended from the map that originally accompanied the *Shan Hai Jing*.

Dr. Hendon M. Harris, Jr.

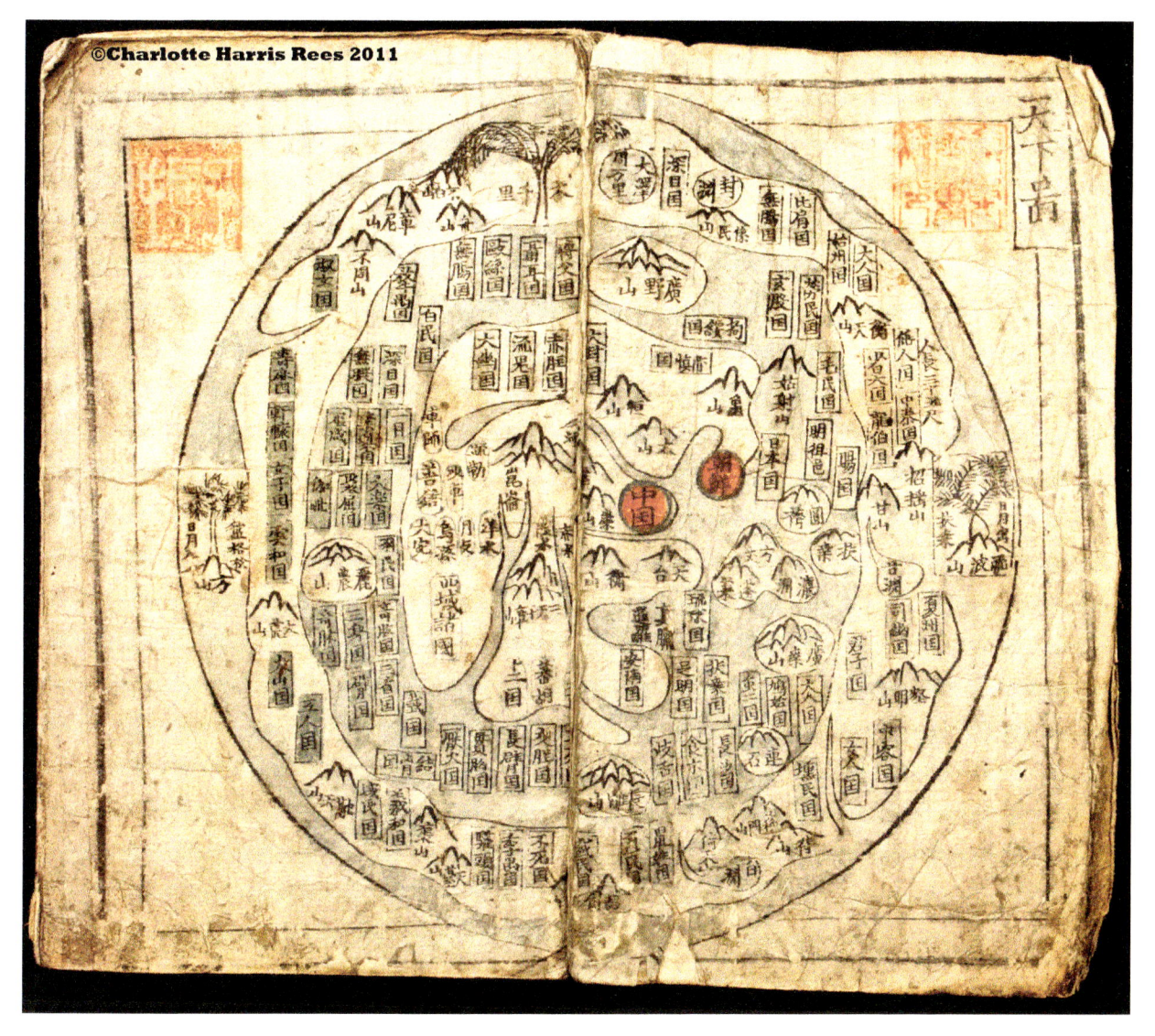

Tian Xia Map from the Dr. Hendon M. Harris, Jr. Collection

- My father and now others identify Fu Sang on the far right side of these world maps as the Americas. In the travels in Fu Sang, the *Shan Hai Jing* mentions a few scattered tribes of people already there.

- According to another Chinese source, some people had been sent to Fu Sang earlier by the Yellow Emperor to study astronomy.

- The *Shan Hai Jing* was held in high regard throughout much of China's history. For many years knowledge of the *Shan Hai Jing* was part of China's civil service exams.

- Some small parts of the *Shan Hai Jing* may have been slightly altered during the many times it was copied over thousands of years. Some commentary was later inserted and is now embedded in the text. This is shown in brackets. The few parts which seem fictitious may have been inserted by copyists or perhaps we just do not yet understand them.

- In the AD 5th century an edict was issued in China to condense all books. Therefore, the account we now have of the *Shan Hai Jing* may well be an abridged version.
- Currently the origin date of the *Shan Hai Jing* is debated. It was quoted many times through China's history. Chao-shi, who lived during the Han Dynasty (202 BC – AD 9) attributed the *Shan Hai Jing* to Yu, the first ruler of the Xia Dynasty. If Chao-shi is correct, that would date it to 2000 BC. At a minimum we know that the *Shan Hai Jing* was in existence when quoted by Chao-shi.
- The *Shan Hai Jing* implies arrival to the Americas by sea.
- In 1885 the portion of the *Shan Hai Jing* thought to apply to North America was published in English by Edward Payson Vining in *An Inglorious Columbus*. For my studies I used Vining's English translation. Mertz wrote that she consulted with a person from the Library of Congress concerning this translation. I also had Vining's translation reviewed by the National Library of China for accuracy and was told that it was "mainly correct," but I have been unsuccessful in getting them to tell me what parts of the translation may be incorrect.

In each chapter of this book which outlines this journey I quote Vining and Mertz then give my own commentary. In bold I have highlighted key words in Vining's text. The reader will find the same words in bold in my commentary as I mention each topic.

The premises listed above are discussed in more detail in my books: *Secret Maps of the Ancient World* (2008, 2009), *Chinese Sailed to America Before Columbus: More Secrets from the Dr. Hendon M. Harris, Jr. Map Collection* (2011), in my 2006 abridgement of my father's 1973 *The Asiatic Fathers of America,* and on my web site www.AsiaticFathers.com.

1 – An American Mystery

We started the trip of the eastern slope of the US Rocky Mountains with a few travel books. However, because of interesting new materials gathered on the way, my backpack became very heavy. As we checked in at the airport on our way home my suitcase was overweight. To satisfy the airline, another large book was moved to my backpack. However, I did not care. I tingled with excitement because of all that we had learned and uncovered on the trip.

It was the day before the first Presidential Debate of 2012 which was to be held in Denver. The long line through security at that airport stretched on and on so Dave reached over to carry the backpack for me. I had to chuckle when he grumbled: "You brought along the whole Library of Congress!"

Several weeks later I confessed to Dave that there had also been a few small stones in the bottom of that backpack that I had collected during my travels.

"Why?" He asked with puzzled consternation.

"Because they're pretty."

Before I settled into my seat on the plane, I took out *The Archaeology of Colorado* at which previously I had only glanced. In my original scan of that text, it caught my eye that Olivella shells were found in some ancient graves in Colorado. They were thought to have come all the way from the Gulf of California and were one of the first trade items of Native Americans. Olivella shells look strikingly similar to tiny cowrie shells, found in some of the most ancient Chinese graves. The Chinese geography, the *Shan Hai Jing*, even mentions cowrie shells off the coast of what has been charted as California. I had no idea about the exciting information ahead.

The Archaeology of Colorado told about an unexplained people group, who for lack of a better name were called the McKean Complex. They visited that area around 4000 years ago.

I was struck with how much the McKean Complex paralleled the Chinese of the same era. The McKean campsite structures were circular and three meters in diameter with packed down earth floor. Their signature was that they contained a basin shaped hearth. They were typically built on river terraces. Some were pit houses.

Did Ancient Chinese Explore America?

The houses of the Chinese Yang-shao villages of that time were also typically three to five meters in diameter and were square, oblong, or round with plastered floors. Each house was furnished with a gourd-shaped pit for a hearth. They were also built on river terraces. Some were pit houses. Archeological drawings of reconstructed Chinese houses of that era look similar to Native American tipis.[1]

The McKean people collected seeds and vegetable products, trapped small animals, and hunted bison. In seeking quartzite, they dug many pits up to thirty feet deep and fifty feet in diameter.[2] At some sites there were mortars and pestles of stone used for processing food. It is a mystery how the McKean people could have been so advanced.

The University of Manitoba stated concerning the McKean Complex:

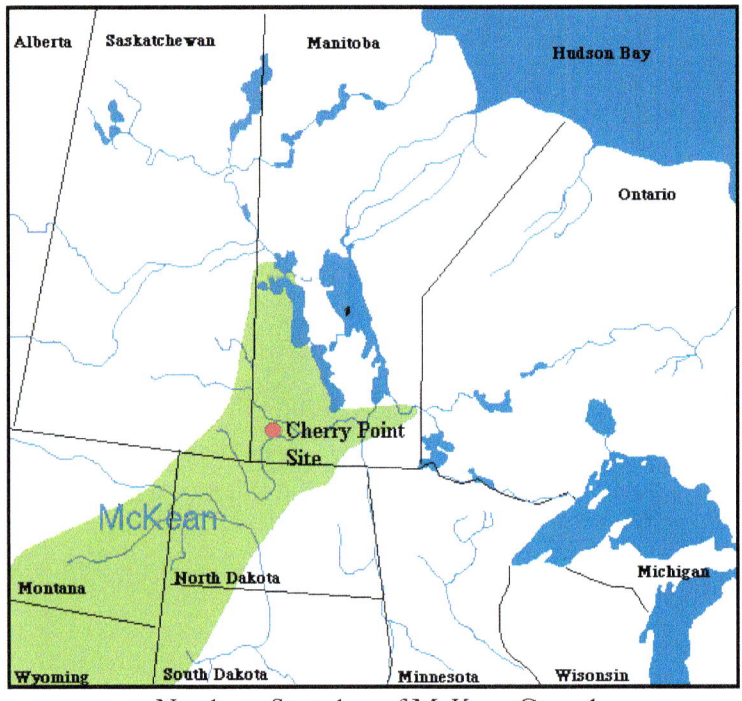

Bone implements that were possibly used for gaming, decorative beads, and basket fragments suggest a complex and elaborate cultural tradition.[3]

The University of Manitoba's map of the northern stretches of the McKean complex showed that this culture spread in a swath from Wyoming north through eastern Montana, western North Dakota, through the southeastern corner of Saskatchewan, and to the south western part of Manitoba, Canada.

Northern Stretches of McKean Complex
by permission of L. Larcombe, University of Manitoba

The outline of the McKean habitation area shown on the map looked strangely familiar. Where had I seen that layout before? Then it dawned on me that it matched one of the journeys of the *Shan Hai Jing* as charted by Mertz. One could almost trace one map from the other.

Most likely Mertz had no knowledge of the McKean Complex when she drew her sketch of that journey. Most of the information for this complex was gathered since

1 – An American Mystery

her book was written and to my knowledge she never mentioned McKean Complex in her writings.

It was noted that only one McKean burial site was found in Canada. That would be typical of a survey group. They would have only taken those who were young and physically fit and would not have stayed a long time.

The journey described in *Shan Hai Jing* Book 4 section 2 for which Mertz had drawn the map similar to the one for the McKean Complex, probably came after the journey described in *Shan Hai Jing* Book 4 section 1, that my husband and I had just followed. However, at some points those two journeys covered the same ground.

Possibly there were different Chinese survey groups for those two journeys who unwittingly crossed paths. The journey similar to the McKean Complex worked south from Manitoba, but on the way also came close to Casper and Medicine Bow Peak in Wyoming and Longs Peak, and the Collegiate Mountains in Colorado. Both surveys seemed to follow the rivers and the mountain ranges.

In Wyoming's Big Horn Mountains, through which Mertz charted this journey, is now a mysterious US federally recognized historic landmark, Big Horn Medicine Wheel, which some refer to as the "American Stonehenge." In the past some tried to explain it by comparing it to an Indian medicine lodge. However, there are several dissimilarities.

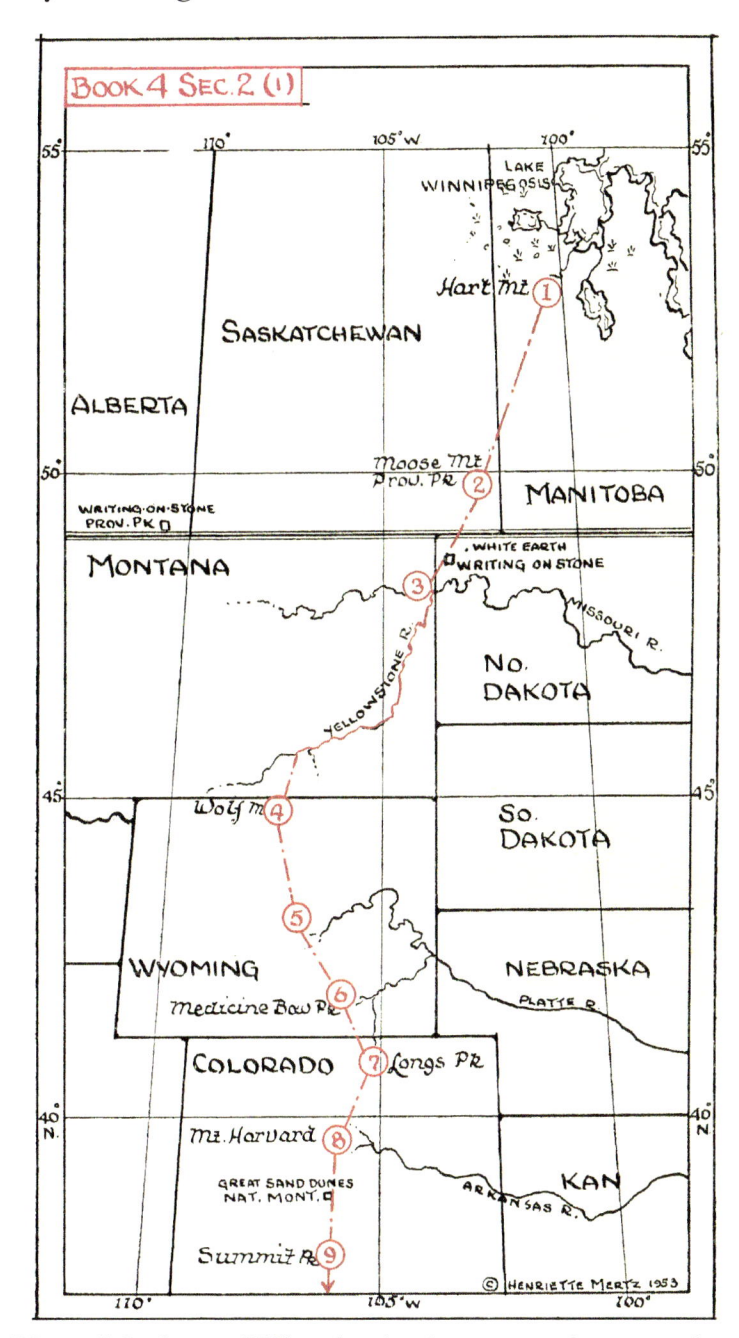

- 3 -

Big Horn Medicine Wheel – Courtesy National Park Service (NPS)

Astronomer, Dr. John Eddy, wrote in *Science Magazine*:

> The word 'medicine' was used by Indians to mean 'magic' or 'supernatural' and the Medicine Wheel is associated in most accounts with religious use.[4]

Eddy discovered that solstice and stellar alignments are indicated by Big Horn Medicine Wheel. When he tested his hypothesis at the summer solstice in June 1972 and again in 1973, he encountered boot deep snow both times. However, though snow was deep at lower elevations, wind cleared the actual circle on both of those occasions. Eddy stated that only at the summer solstice would there have been practical access.

Stanford University describes it:

> an 80' diameter wheel-like pattern made of stones. At the center of the circle is a doughnut-shaped pile of stones, a cairn, connected to the rim by 28 spoke like lines of stones. Six more stone cairns are arranged around the circle, most large enough to hold a sitting human. The central cairn is about 12 feet in diameter and 2 feet high.[5]

It may be of great significance that Big Horn Medicine Wheel is divided by 28 spokes, not equally spaced apart, with each spoke going out from a hub.

1 – An American Mystery

According to Needham, in the early second millennium BC Chinese divided the night sky into 28 sections to mark the 28 days of the lunar calendar. The spokes on those Chinese star charts were around a hub and purposely were not equidistant.

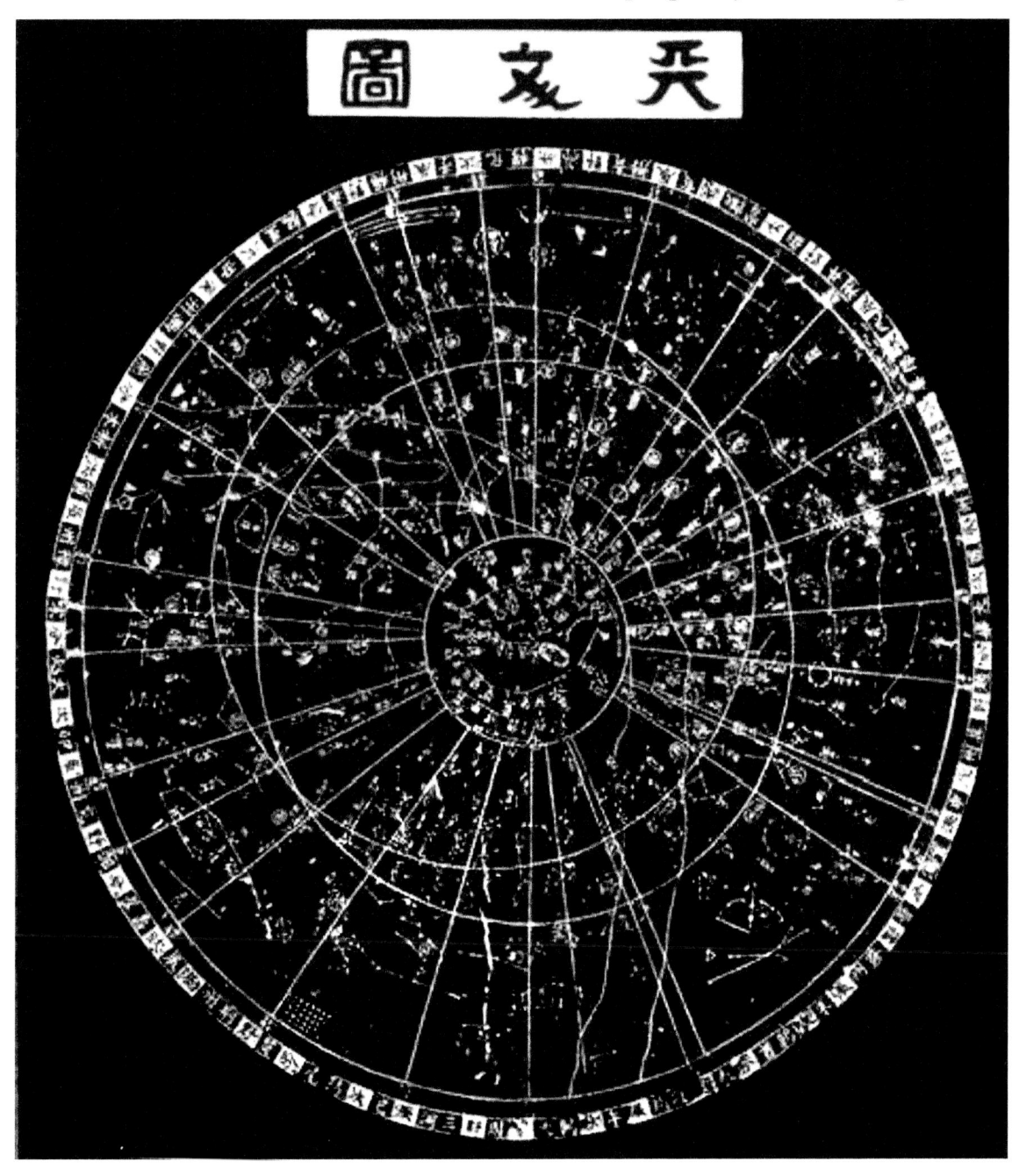

Photo courtesy of Robert Temple author of *The Genius of China*

A photo of one of the Chinese astronomical devices can be seen in the *Genius of China*.[6] It is very similar to the Wyoming model.

It is not possible to carbon date stone, but attempts to date Big Horn Medicine Wheel by objects found nearby gave a date of around AD 1700 – before Caucasians reached that region. However, a problem arises concerning the possibility of Native American construction of it. On its discovery by Caucasians no native group could tell about its origin other than to say that "the Sun built it" or that it had been there from "before the light came." The Crow Indians said it: "was made by people who had no iron."[7] All those statements imply great antiquity.

Centuries later people from India adopted the same lunar system with 28 spokes, but it was the Chinese who initiated it. Chinese astronomical methods were later adopted by the world and are used today. Using the stars Chinese were able to navigate and then return home at early dates.

In fact, Edward Vining in quoting *Kuan-Mei* reported that one reason that Chinese first came to Fu Sang (America) was for astronomical studies. "It is in Fu-sang that Hwang-ti's astronomers resided (who were charged with the observation of the rising sun)."[8] Hwang-ti mentioned here was the legendary Yellow Emperor who preceded the earliest Chinese dynasty.

Even if nomadic Native American tribes, not known for buildings or monuments, did construct Big Horn Medicine Wheel, how did they gain such complicated knowledge of astronomy which enabled them to build a structure that charts not only the progress of the sun but also that of at least three different stars?

In the Big Horn Basin in Wyoming is found some of the oldest rock art in North America – believed to date back thousands of years. Perhaps that should be considered in dating Big Horn Medicine Wheel. Legend Rock, which is downstream from Big Horn Medicine Wheel, has been linked by technique and imagery to sites around the world including Ningxia, China.[9] Similar rock art in China also dates back thousands of years to their early dynasties.[10]

If per chance the Chinese built Big Horn Medicine wheel in Wyoming in the second millennium BC, is it possible that an unsupported structure made of loose stones could survive all those years?

If this were New Mexico, in which Spaniards and others repeatedly explored and warred starting in the early 16th century, probably not. But in Wyoming, which the white men did not reach until the 19th century and in a remote location at almost 10,000 feet altitude on a mountain covered with snow for most of the year, the possibility exists. This is on a well worn trail, but technically very much "off the beaten path."

1 – An American Mystery

There are other similar wheels in the area. University Regina, Saskatchewan reports:

> Boulder monuments are patterns traced upon virgin prairie utilizing glacial till boulders to define a desired outline pattern. The boulders most commonly used range from 10 cm (4 inches) to 40cm (16 inches) in diameter....Currently 167 of these monuments have been recorded in Saskatchewan....examples include 11 medicine wheels, 10 ceremonial circles, four human effigies, five animal effigies, and three geometric designs....An additional 200 - 300 have been recorded on the Northern Great Plains.[11]

The oldest of those monuments in Saskatchewan has been tentatively dated at 1600 years old. Northern Great Plains locations which they listed include Montana, South Dakota, Wyoming, Minnesota, and Iowa. Again note that these were mainly locations on which Mertz charted *Shan Hai Jing* journeys.

In *Chinese Maritime Activities and Socioeconomic Development, c. 2100 B.C. – 1900 A.D.* Dr. Gang (Kent) Deng of the London School of Economics cites many different authors who illustrate that Chinese had gone to sea by this early period.

Dr. Kwang-Chih Chang of Harvard wrote in two of his books about peanuts (Arachis hypogaea), native to the Americas, found in archeological sites in two different provinces in China that dated to before 2000 BC.[12] Dr. Nasir El Bassan, confirms that Arachis hypogaea is native to tropical and subtropical South America.[13] That is further indication that Chinese crossed the Pacific at early dates.

However, the mysteries seemingly remain. Who were those advanced McKean Complex people? Who built the medicine wheels and when? In the early and mid 20th century American archeologists went to Europe to try to find answers to mysteries about Native Americans. Still today, many will not show the same interest in looking across the Pacific for the solution.

2 – Casper, Wyoming

The beginning of the "Classic of the Eastern Mountains" says that SUH-CHU Mountain on its northern side adjoins KAN-MEI Mountain (or **Sunless Mountain**). **SHIH River (or "drinkable water")** is found here, a stream that flows northeasterly into the sea. In it there are many water animals called **YUNG-YUNG**. These look like brindled cattle [i. e., they resemble cattle that are striped like tigers]. Their voices sound like the grunting of swine. (Vining translation of *Shan Hai Jing* Book 4 Section 1.)

Mertz Note:

A peak (5930 ft.) twenty miles due west of Casper, Wyoming appears to be SUH-CHU Mountain. On its northern side, it adjoins the Big Horn Range. SHIH River (or drinkable water) is the Sweetwater River which here joins the North Platte and flows northeasterly, eventually into the Mississippi and the sea. The animals, which in color are like brindled cattle, are probably beaver or otter.[14]

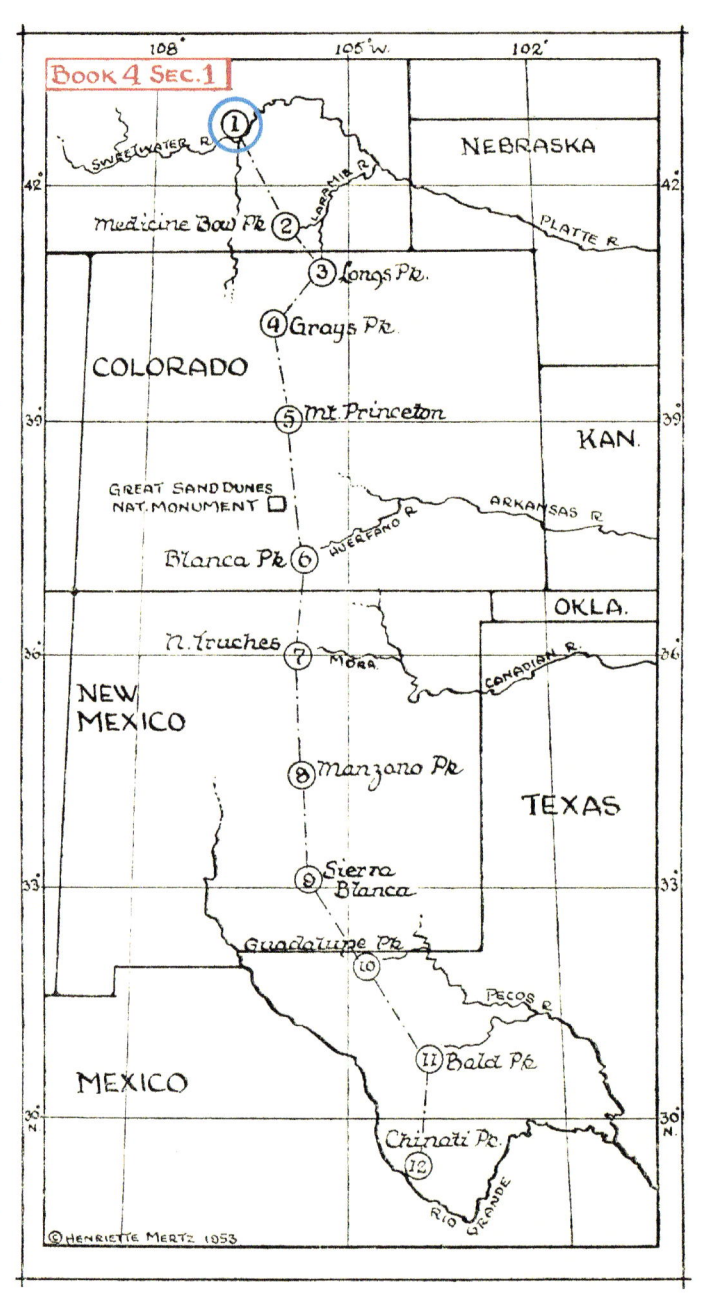

I have…used Vining for basic translation purposes, supplemented by consultations with the same Chinese scholar at the Library of Congress who assisted me with translation of Fu-sang and Kingdom of Women. In chapter XXXV of *An Inglorious*

Columbus, Vining prints his own translation of the portion of the Classics of the Mountains and Seas used here. Bracketed notations throughout are part of the Chinese text as it appears in the Classics; the notes were put there at an early date by a scholar who, no doubt was trying to locate the mountains and rivers in China. Parenthetical notations are Vining's. Each "Note" section is my own interpretation of the Chinese text.[15]

Author's Comments:

Dave and I live in Virginia. For this trip we flew out in early morning. Just after 9 a.m. (two hours time difference) we arrived in Denver and picked up our rental car for our drive north to Wyoming where we would begin our survey. Our first stop was a museum in Denver to check the display of gems. It was not because we were going gem hunting. It was that I was having a serious inner conflict. Mertz contended that there was jade in Colorado, yet in my research I could find no such evidence. I wondered if the journey my husband and I were about to undertake was just a pipe dream.

In fact, this whole trip was almost cancelled at the last moment. When I calculated how much money we would spend on the two weeks of travel, I quickly checked out locations in the Caribbean. For the same amount of money we could have had a lovely vacation there.

Truthfully I was tired, too. My presentations in 2012 had taken me to Canada, Switzerland, London, Washington DC, California, and most recently Hong Kong and Nanjing. The thought of time on a quiet beach was very tempting. However, it was Dave who insisted that we follow through with our *Shan Hai Jing* trip since I had wanted to do it for so long. It was September and if we waited much longer, some areas would be inaccessible because of snow.

As we drove north from Denver the terrain looked very different from our part of Virginia which gets much rain and is verdant green with plants and trees. In northern Colorado and into Wyoming we were looking at bare land with little vegetation. We could see many interesting details of the rocks, normally not visible in our area. Each hillock we passed took us into another fascinating zone.

We had reservations at C'mon Inn in Casper which was constructed from huge timbers and colorful boulders. In the interior roofed courtyard are a swimming pool and five hot tubs. A waterfall and stuffed wild animals including antelope, peccary, and a wolf provide decorations. Both the evening of our arrival and the next morning we enjoyed the hot tubs and swimming pool.

Did Ancient Chinese Explore America?

C'mon Inn in Casper

In the morning we visited the National Historic Trails Interpretive Center in Casper to learn more about the California, Oregon, and Mormon trails which passed through this area. For those who traveled west by foot following their covered wagons, this was a long and arduous journey filled with many dangers and often death. Once the transcontinental railroad went through, the trip that had taken six months of walking from Independence, Missouri to the West was reduced to less than a week.

The National Park Service writes:

> The Rocky Mountains stretch like a jagged spine between Alaska and Mexico, splitting North America into East and West. The Continental Divide is not a simple line of peaks, easily thread by tracks and roads, but a complex of overlapping mountain ranges and treeless sagebrush steppe, hundreds of miles wide. In the days of covered wagon travel, the Rockies were an imposing barrier to the movement of people, commerce, and communications.[16]

At a rest stop on Highway 220 west of Casper in Natrona County, we viewed Independence Rock. The Sweetwater River flows right by this enormous boulder.

Today not far from where the Sweetwater meets the North Platte River there is a man made reservoir. However, the North Platte still continues north from there.

This is also the area charted by Mertz as the start of this *Shan Hai Jing* journey. Near the continental divide and far from either coast, to me at first it seemed a strange place for a Chinese party to start surveys of North America.

If the *Shan Hai Jing* journeys were in fact real, the Chinese had to first travel inland for hundreds of miles to get here. How did they come? Even though this is listed first among the four specific surveys of North America in the *Shan Hai Jing*, I believe that it probably came after two other journeys which Mertz charted on or closer to the West Coast.

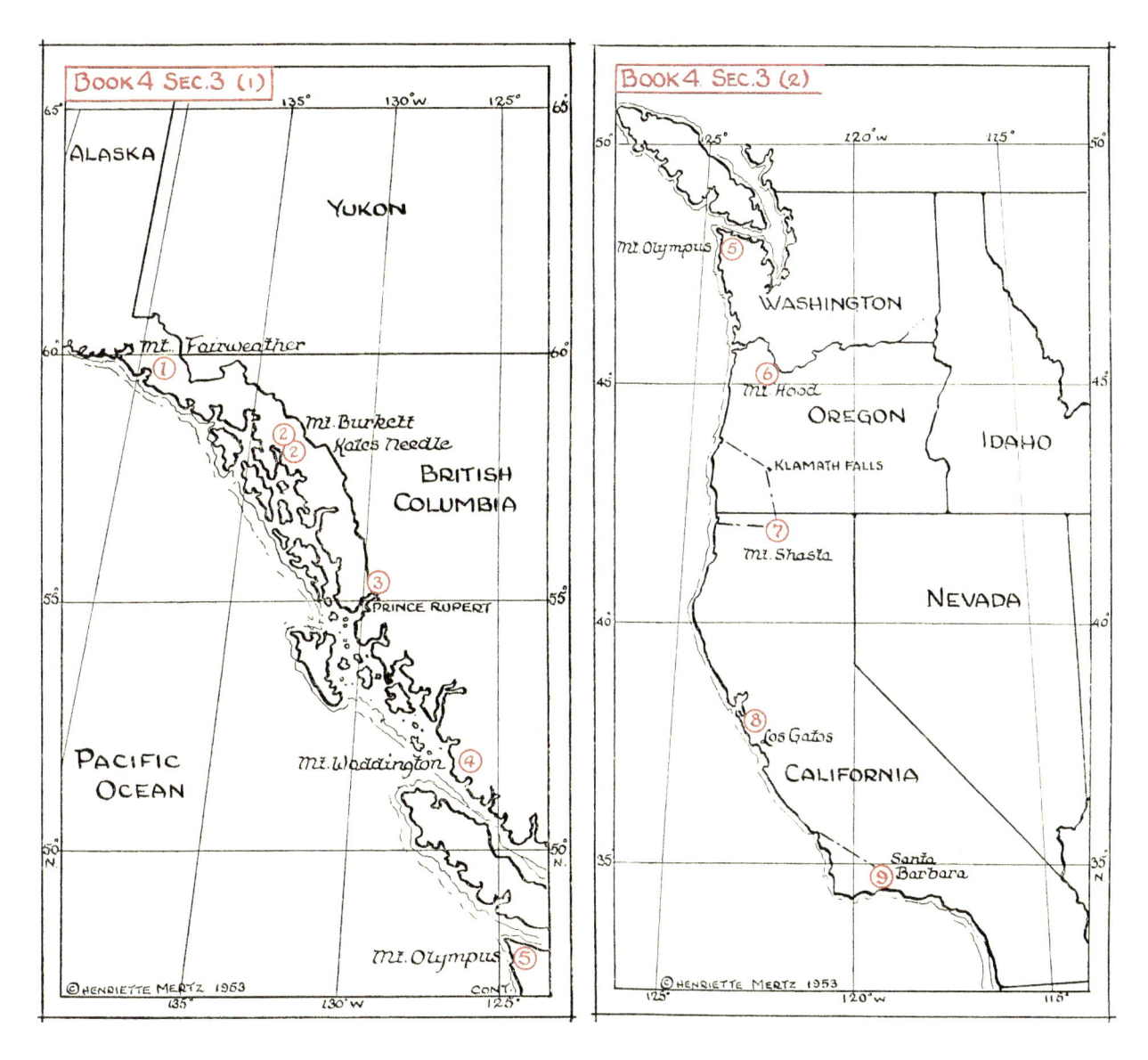

One of the four ancient surveys (*Shan Hai Jing* Book 4 Section 3) started at Mt. Fairweather, on the border of Alaska, US, and British Columbia, Canada. That trek follows the West Coast of North America down to Santa Barbara, California. It correctly describes geography and locates some animals native to North America.

It seems only logical that this area on the North American West Coast would have been the Chinese "port of entry" and that they arrived by sea – especially since the *Shan Hai Jing* mentions "the flowing stream" thousands of li long. (A li is about 1/3 mile long.)

This is also where debris from the 2011 Japanese tsunami is currently washing ashore in North America. Two major ocean gyres, the Aleut and the Turtle, are there.[17]

Did Ancient Chinese Explore America?

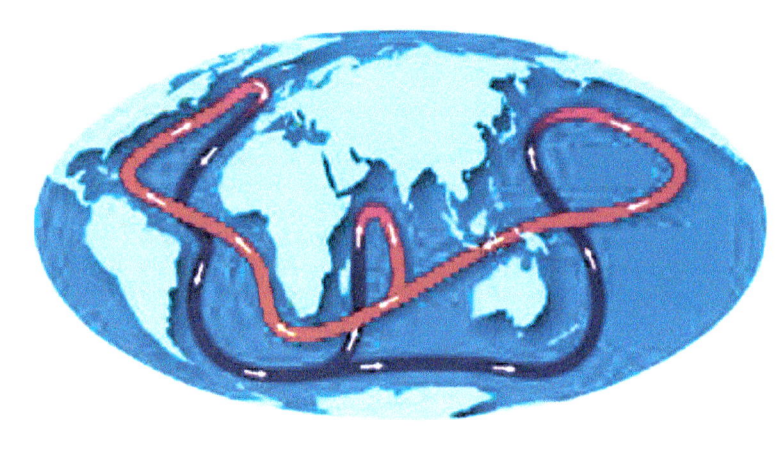

Diagram courtesy of NOAA

They are shaped like race tracks between Asia and North America and back.

They continually act as moving oceanic sidewalks pushing objects across the Pacific.

According to the US National Oceanic and Atmospheric Administration (NOAA), one of those gyres is up to 62 miles (100 kilometers) wide and over .6 mile (1 kilometer) deep.[18] It is a warm current. Numerous accounts relate that people in that current can catch rain water and fish the whole way across. In the 20th century several individuals in very small boats – including a row boat, a raft, and a three person boat – crossed the Pacific using those gyres.[19]

The best-selling book, *Unbroken*, gives the account of two US airmen whose plane went down in the Pacific in World War II. They lived on a life raft and survived for 47 days on rain water and the fish they caught as they drifted 2000 miles on the westward flowing segment of that gyre. Eventually they were captured by the Japanese.

Dr. Joseph Needham of Cambridge University wrote in reference to Chinese knowledge of this current:

> Already in the Warring States period [403-221BC] this great gulf stream perpetually flowing north-eastwards [from Asia] seems to have been known....[20]

Flotsametrics and the Floating World states: "More than twenty-two hundred years ago the Chinese called the Kuroshio by the prescient name Wei Lu..."[21]

Apparently at some time ancient Chinese mariners reached the coast of California. Bob Meistrell, founder of BodyGlove (wet suits), while diving there, found about 30 round anchors of the style used by ancient Chinese. He was

Bob Meistrell with ancient Chinese style boat anchors

- 12 -

told that judging from the chemical accumulation on them they had been on the sea bed 3,000 to 4,000 years. His friend Wayne Baldwin also found a similar anchor. The anchor on the left in this photo broke in half as it was hoisted up. Bob said the whole anchor would have weighed a ton.

According to Mertz, another of the four surveys (*SHJ* Book 4, Section 4) started at Mt. Rainer, Washington. A few miles inland from the Pacific, this journey moved south ending in northern Nevada near the southwest corner of Idaho. This location in Nevada is not far from where, many years later, the California trail stretched as it followed an ancient path.

Outside of Casper by Independence Rock, Dave and I were delighted to still be able to see tracks from the covered wagons of the almost 500,000 American emigrants who traveled through that area between 1843 and 1869.

At this location in Wyoming the Oregon Trail, the California Trail, the Mormon Trail, and the Pony Express all followed the same path. The Oregon and California trails each stretched for around 2000 miles from Missouri to their respective destinations on the western frontier.

Thousands of those emigrants carved or painted their names on Independence Rock. It was a celebratory time to reach this half way point and it was perhaps the most noted landmark on that trail. Standing 700 feet wide, 1900 feet long, and 128 feet high, Independence Rock was impos-sible to miss. If they reached it by Independence Day (July 4) they should be able to make it through the mountains ahead before winter.

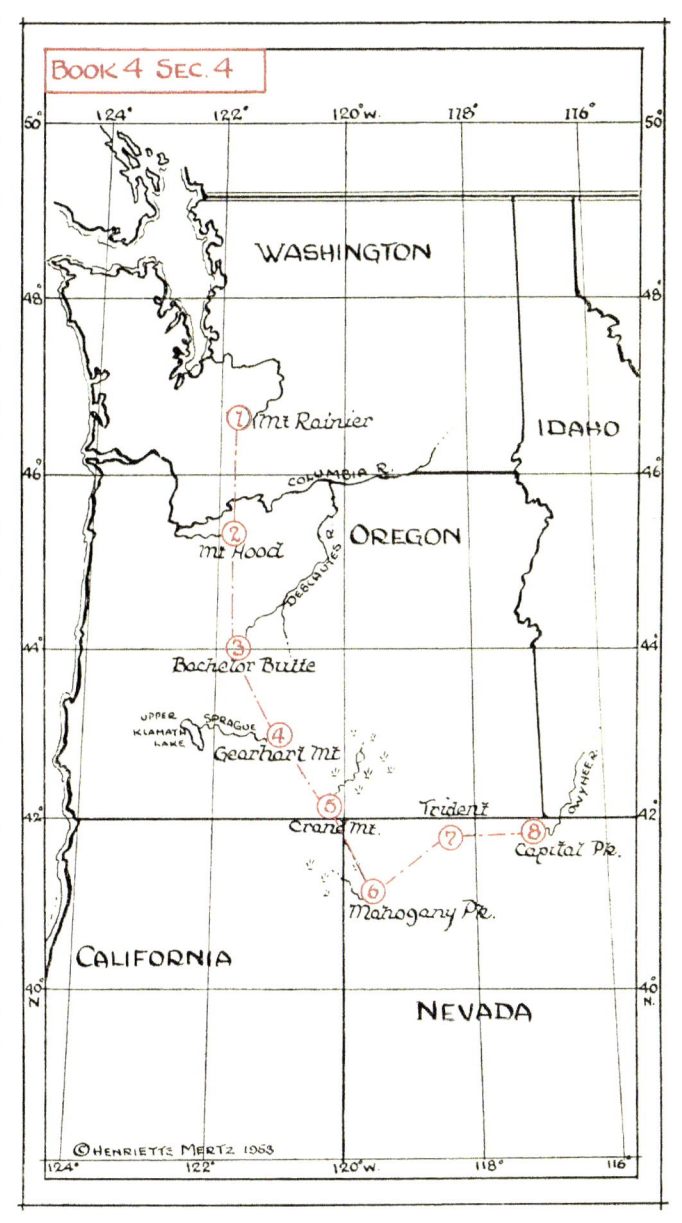

Did Ancient Chinese Explore America?

This was the beginning of the South Pass which was the next 100 miles of climb to cross the Continental Divide. During that ascent those following this route would have to cross the Sweetwater River nine times. This pass was the only way through the mountains that was wide enough for a wagon.

Independence Rock in Wyoming

Today Independence Rock still stands with majesty. Most of the names once carved or painted on it are now weathered, but a few can still be read. Further west and through the pass, the groups from the 1800s split to go on to Oregon, California, or Utah.

The earliest Caucasians who traveled overland to the West Coast did not know this route so their journeys were extremely difficult. It was only when some travelers were returning east that they were told by an Indian how to find and follow this old trace.

The National Park Service states:

> South Pass was the gateway to the West. Without that accident of geography, there would have been no Oregon Trail, no California Trail, no Mormon Utah, and perhaps no United States stretching from the Atlantic to the Pacific."[22]

Perhaps years earlier the Chinese walked one of those same trails, traveling in the opposite direction, from west to east. When I realized that this was the only good pass through the mountains, it made perfect sense why the Chinese started their survey of the eastern side of the Rocky Mountains there near Casper, Wyoming.

The Chinese name "**SHIH**," translated "**Drinkable Water**," for the river at this location may give us another clue about how they arrived. Why would people in that era name any river "drinkable" unless they had recently encountered other water that was not potable?

The map of Wyoming indicates that other waterways west of this area include Muddy Creek, Bitter Creek, Sandy River and the brackish Salt River. Just west of the pass was two days of travel without fresh water.[23] The rivers to the east of Independence Rock were drinkable. Therefore, the Chinese most likely arrived from the west. One can imagine a parched traveler tentatively sipping from the Sweetwater River then joyously proclaiming to the others: "Drinkable water!"

According to the *World Atlas* it is unusual for any river in the world to run north. To do so it must run downhill. You will note in this journey that the Chinese mention several north flowing rivers in correct sequence.

I am still not sure what might have been meant by the Chinese mention of "**sunless mountain**" near here. I wondered how a mountain could be sunless unless the sun was somehow blocked.

Visible from Independence Rock is Devil's Gate, a very narrow pass through the mountains just north. The road does not go through Devil's Gate, but we stopped and could see that Devil's Gate was dark and shaded. Perhaps that was what the *Shan Hai Jing* implied.

The National Park Service stated:

> Devil's Gate is among the more interesting geographical landmarks along the emigrant trails. This natural feature became visible approximately 15 miles to the east. The gorge was impassable to wagons, and the trail passed to the south of the ridge, but this dark, gloomy canyon intrigued the emigrants. Many camped here and almost all took the detour to inspect the gorge.
>
> Osborne Cross recorded on July 10, 1949: "This gap is truly wonderful, being a space not over twenty yards wide and about five hundred feet high, having very much the appearance of being chiseled out by the hand of man rather than the work of nature."[24]

Devil's Gate - Ryan Reeder photo

Today most contend that the gorge was carved by the Sweetwater River.

> The Shoshone and Arapahoe Indians attribute Devil's Gate to the actions of an evil beast with enormous tusks that once roamed this area, preventing the Indians from hunting and camping in this region. Eventually the Indians became disgusted and decided to kill the beast. From the passes and

ravines the warriors shot the beast with a multitude of arrows. The beast, enraged, tore a hole in the mountains with his large tusks and escaped.[25]

On this trip we visited museums with displays of enormous dinosaurs and mastodons whose bones were found in that part of the US. The bones have gone to many different museums around the world. According to *History of Wyoming*, one triceratops skull weighed 3650 pounds when boxed up for a museum.[26] One house in Wyoming is even made out of dinosaur bones.

My first night in Wyoming, after visiting a museum, I dreamed about dinosaurs. After those nightmares, it is easy for me to sympathize with the Native American account of how Devil's Gate might have been formed.

Pronghorn Courtesy NPS

I could not accept Mertz's explanation that **YUNG-YUNG,** the animals in this location that looked like striped cattle, were beavers or otters. My first thought was of zebras, but immediately realized that they would not be in North America. I looked through many books on North American animals and was almost convinced that no striped animal the size of cattle lived in North America.

Then I came across a photo of a pronghorn which has stripes across its chest. Perhaps because of their scientific name, Antilocapra Americana, many people refer to them as antelope. To my great excitement I learned that they run wild in Wyoming today.

Adult pronghorn bucks usually weigh between 90 and 120 pounds. Females weigh about 20 pounds less. That is much closer to the size of cattle than beavers, which Mertz guessed the Chinese to be describing. Therefore, I believe that the early Chinese explorers were describing pronghorn which are native to North America.

On our trip to Casper and to the Sweetwater River we saw numerous pronghorn along the highways. In fact, it is estimated that today there are more pronghorn than people in Wyoming. Though they are usually found on land, I found photos on the internet of pronghorn coming out of water as the Chinese described. They do occasionally make a soft grunting sound.

These animals are mentioned in the famous American song "Home on the Range" by Dr. Brewster M. Higley of Kansas:

Pronghorn Courtesy NPS

Give me a home where the buffalo roam and the deer and the antelope play. Where seldom is heard a discouraging word and the skies are not cloudy all day.[27]

Because of the drought and recent fires in the area, the Wyoming skies at times were hazy, but like the song mentions there were few clouds. I used sunscreen, but my skin still turned bright red.

We also saw many buffalo (bison). Featured on the Wyoming state flag, bison no longer roam wild, but today are raised on farms. One would have thought that if the Chinese were in Wyoming they would have also mentioned bison. However, I recognized no mention of them in this Chinese text.

As I discussed in *Chinese Sailed to America before Columbus,* bison and horses are listed on the US Great Plains on the Chinese 1602 world map *Kunyu wangou quantu (Map of Ten Thousand Countries of the Earth)*.[28] That map was produced over 200 years before Lewis and Clark, the first Caucasian explorers to that area, went there. That information had to have come from before 1433, when China shut itself off from the rest of the world.

My research mentor, Dr. Covey, reminded me that at one time all the books in China were abridged. What is left of the *Shan Hai Jing* is most likely not the full account that was written at the time. Perhaps that is why I found no mention of bison.

3 – Medicine Bow Peak, Wyoming

And it says that, three hundred li to the south, LEI Mountain (or Mountain of **Creeping Plants**) is to be found. Upon this there are **gems and** below it there is **gold**. **HU River** is found here, a stream that **flows easterly into SHIH River**. In this there are many **HWOH-SHI**. [These are **tadpoles**; the book entitled the RH'-YA calls them HWOH-TUNG.] (Vining translation of *Shan Hai Jing*)

Mertz Note:

Three hundred li is approximately equivalent to one hundred miles – a Chinese li is just a fraction under one third of a statute mile. One hundred miles due south, Medicine Bow Peak (12,005 feet) is found. Gold and semi-precious gems are plentiful in the area. The Hu River is a small tributary flowing down the eastern slope of Medicine Bow Peak emptying into the Laramie which flows easterly into the North Platte.

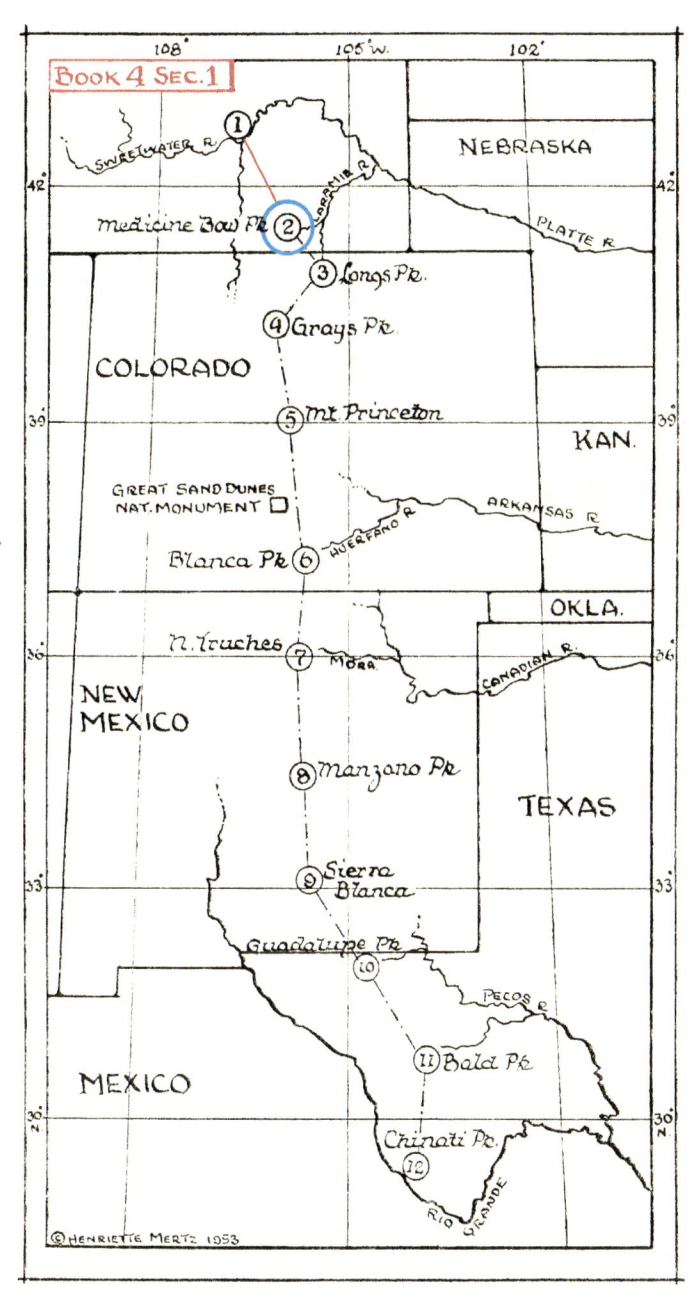

Author's Comments:

From Independence Rock we drove to our next destination, Medicine Bow Peak, Wyoming. About 20 miles west of Independence Rock we turned south at

Did Ancient Chinese Explore America?

Highway 287. The north flowing North Platte River is only a few miles east of Route 287, and I believe that is how the ancient Chinese, if they were indeed here, would have traveled going upstream on that river.

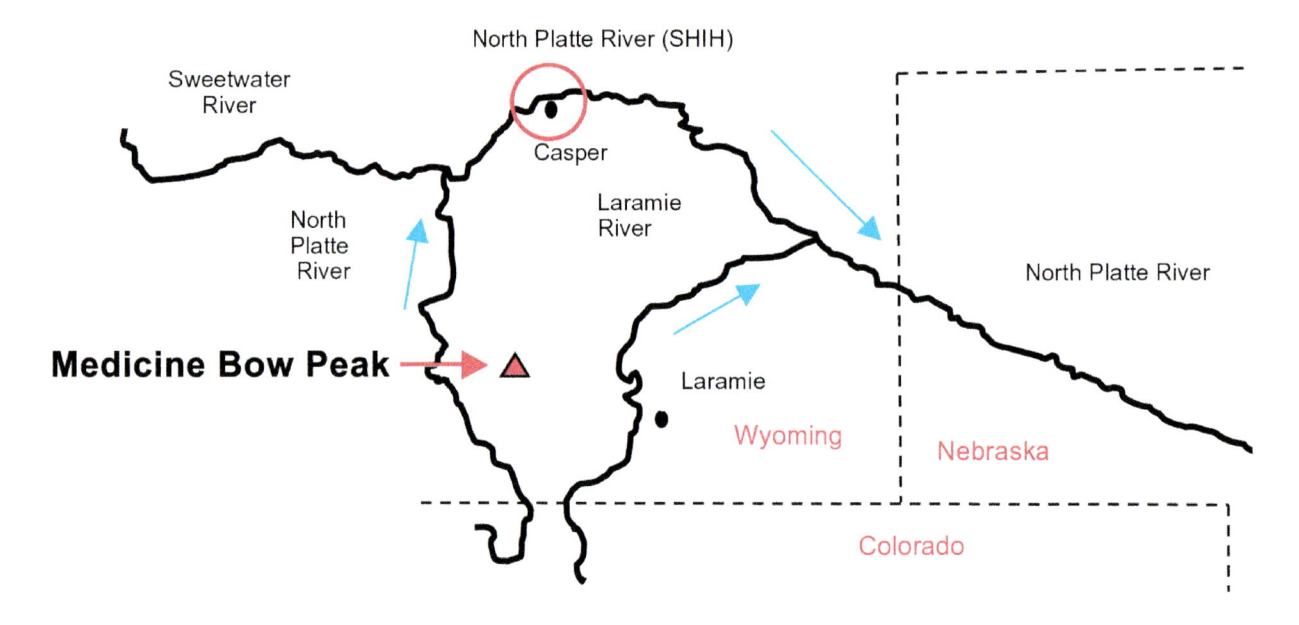

Medicine Bow Peak, Wyoming

The north flowing **SHIH River** was mentioned by the Chinese both at Medicine Bow Peak and at the Casper location. They knew that the same river connected the two locations as the North Platte River does.

While traveling south we were parallel to the North Platte, which is to the west of Medicine Bow Peak. Therefore, at first I was perplexed about how the stream from Medicine Bow Peak could flow east and hit the North Platte. However, the North Platte flows north and then east. Different sections of the North Platte are west, north, or northeast of Medicine Bow Peak.

Water runs east from Medicine Bow Mountains into a tributary of the Laramie River (**Hu River**). Further northeast the Laramie flows into the North Platte.

At one time the Laramie River was teaming with tadpoles, as the Chinese stated. The **HWOH-SHI tadpoles** are surely those of Wyoming toads (Bufo baxteri). According to Amphibian Rescue and Conservation

Wyoming Toad
Photo by and courtesy of Amy Hopperstad USFWS

project the Wyoming toad: "…once was one of the most plentiful vertebrate species in the Laramie River Basin Wyoming."[29]

This is the only part of the world where this type of toad is found. Recently they were almost extinct, but since 1995 more than 100,000 tadpoles and toads have been re-introduced. However, in this exact location the Chinese reported many tadpoles.

Driving south from Independence Rock we passed signs marking the North American Continental Divide several times, though at that time we were still on open prairie and not yet into the mountains. For many miles we saw few indications of civilization other than the road.

The Continental Divide Trail, administered by the National Park Service, stretches 3100 miles from Canada to Mexico. This trail runs nearby and parallel to Highway 287, and then on to Medicine Bow National Forest.

It is ironic that this meandering trail runs close to or over the first five locations charted by Mertz for this survey. One might suspect that Mertz purposely chose locations on the Continental Divide Trail. Although many of the trails were there from long ago, the Continental Divide Trail did not receive its national designation until 1978 – decades after Mertz wrote her book.

Part of the Continental Divide Trail

As we were driving my thoughts went back to a brief phone conversation I had several years ago with a man who told me he had found Chinese writing on an object in Wyoming. The man said that he had previously worked with Mel Fisher in finding gold on sunken treasure ships.

At the time we talked, the man was living in Wyoming. Using satellite imagery he located a very old trail on his property which was not visible at ground level.

Thinking that perhaps it was a north-south bound Aztec Indian trail, he followed it hoping to find gold. However, instead he found the object with Chinese inscription.

Wyoming is the least populated state in the union with less than 6 people per square mile.[30] Many people there enjoy solitude and want to be left alone. This man was only interested in what I might know about Chinese in Wyoming and never would give me any more proof or information, nor would he continue our dialogue. While I have not been able to verify his account, he was introduced to me by someone I consider credible.

Guided by a travel book about Wyoming, we pressed on in order to reach a US Forest Service ranger station in the hamlet of Centennial before it closed for the day. I had questions to ask about the Medicine Bow Peak area. Unfortunately, our rush was in vain. Upon arriving we learned that the ranger station there had been closed a couple of years. We had to try to find other ways to obtain answers for some of our questions.

Fifty types of dinosaurs have been unearthed in Wyoming. In our rush to get to the ranger station we missed taking a side trip to see the museum made out of 5,776 dinosaur bones weighing 102,000 pounds (46,364 kilos).[31] Jade is the state gem of Wyoming. We had also missed seeing the world longest jade bar which is 40 feet long and cut from a Wyoming boulder weighing four and a half tons.[32] However, on Highway 130 into Centennial we saw a huge ranch of wild horses.

The mountains near Centennial are known as Snowy Range. Highway 130 is a scenic byway and Wyoming's second highest pass. The map alerts motorists that at times this road is closed because of snow. It is typically open June through October, weather permitting.

Centennial (population 270) was interesting. We had chosen to spend the night there because of its proximity to Medicine Bow Peak. The advertisement on the internet for Old Corral Hotel & Steak House where we stayed stated:

> In 1875 a group of hunters came across pure gold outcroppings sticking right out of the ground in the Snowy Range Mountains just a few hundred yards to our west.

Sure enough, almost next door to the hotel was the train depot where the railroad line ended. It had been built to fetch the gold, but did not appear to still be in use. On the other side of the hotel only yards away the mountains sharply ascended. We saw no gold, but bright yellow aspens glittered in the sunlight.

3 – Medicine Bow Peak, Wyoming

A rich gold vein was mined right there until 1877 when it hit a fault. They never could determine where the vein continued and since then no one with modern equipment has really tried.[33]

We soon discovered that folks in Centennial have a relaxed mentality. Even though it was only 4:30 p.m. when we arrived and had a confirmed reservation, the hotel office was closed as well as the advertised steak house.

Entering an open side door to the hotel, we walked down the hall. We wondered if perhaps the hotel was deserted and were about to leave when we saw a lady who said that she and her husband were staying there, too. She had seen our room keys by the back door in an envelope with our name on it.

We let ourselves in and spent the night in the clean and comfortable room with rustic western style furniture made out of huge logs. However, without the password from the hotel staff, we could not check the internet to answer our questions. The next morning a hotel staff person was there when we paid our bill and checked out.

Not only was the steak house with the hotel closed, but a second restaurant as well. The next day the library, which we were assured contained information about area mining, had still not opened up even 30 minutes after its posted starting time.

There was one restaurant that opened for the evening meal and another (Friendly's) for breakfast.

A sheriff's car sat in front of Friendly's with "911" on its side, but had flat tires and grass growing up around it. Apparently the crime rate in that area is very low.

In Centennial I discovered silver – a dime in the gravel parking lot.

Medicine Bow Peak at Sunrise

At night the stars shone brightly across the sky. We rose before dawn to take photos of Medicine Bow Peak at daybreak from a recommended location at 11,000 feet elevation. The early morning light turned the quartzite mountains, which normally look white, to beautiful shades of pink.

It was cold so we had dressed warmly. Below and between us and Medicine Bow Peak was Lake Marie at 10,600 feet. To the south we could faintly see Longs Peak approximately 100 miles away and our next stop on this *Shan Hai Jing* journey.

I tried to imagine what the Chinese were describing as the **creeping plant** for which they named the mountain. Medicine Bow itself is above the tree line and I saw no plants there. However, signs where Dave and I stood to take photos indicated that moss campion

Moss Campion – Courtesy of NPS

(Silene acaulis) there grew only half an inch in five years, so not to step on it. Some of these wild plants there are 100 years old. In the summer they bloom profusely in shades of pink. Could that be what was meant

by "creeping plants"? As we ascended and descended the mountain from and to our hotel, cattle nonchalantly walked across the road.

Back in Centennial we found Friendly's open for breakfast. I decided to ask other customers, who we guessed might be locals, what they knew about minerals found in the area. A group of old timers told me that there were lots of claims for various minerals, but they were not big enough for companies to take on the mining projects. The mining in Centennial itself had dried up years ago. These people were mainly retirees. A man came in and was introduced for the first time to an older gentleman. The older gentleman replied, "I don't come into town much."

My mind raced. In what remote location did this older man live that he thought Centennial was "town"?

When I told them that I was researching about whether ancient Chinese had visited that area, one man pointed to a plaque on the wall which said something to the effect: "In 1792 when only the Indians lived here absolutely nothing of importance happened." Feeling a racist overtone, I decided not to tell anyone else for the rest of my trip the purpose of my questions.

My brother Hendon had asked us to check out Cinnabar Park near Medicine Bow Peak. It is down a bumpy gravel road and near to Rob Roy Reservoir. On the way we passed through a hamlet where the road sign read: "Albany, population 15."

Hendon had seen stripes in the vicinity of Cinnabar Park on Google Maps and wondered what they were. As it turned out, the stripes were where logging had recently been done in long strips. Cinnabar was used both by the Native Americans and the Chinese to make red paint, but I never could find out how the park – now just a large grassy lot – got its name.

Gold was found near Cinnabar Park. Some of the gravel in the road there was a reddish color. On the way we spotted a bald eagle on a fence post.

Did Ancient Chinese Explore America?

Lake Marie near Medicine Bow Peak

Moose live in the Snowy Range and I had hoped to see one, but we did not. As we looked back at Medicine Bow Peak, now in full sun, it glinted white as if covered with snow.

Even though the Indian Bathtubs near Riverside are just a few miles from Medicine Bow Peak, we did not have time to find them. They are cut four feet deep in granite and were reportedly used in ceremonies and bathing by the Native Americans.[34] We were not exactly sure how to find them and reaching them would have required a one hour hike. Our entire trip was just two weeks long and we had other planned stops before nightfall.

In Laramie we visited the University of Wyoming. I wanted to visit the geology museum there to see the dinosaur exhibits and also their library to read about mining in Medicine Bow Peak area. Unfortunately, their visitors' information center and the dinosaur exhibits were closed for renovations.

The librarians in the Geology Department at the beautiful campus of the University of Wyoming were most helpful. One of the books that the librarians brought to me was *Guide to the Geology, Mining Districts, and Ghost Towns of Medicine Bow*

At University of Wyoming

and Snowy Ridge Scenic Byway by W. Daniel Hausel. It listed **numerous finds of precious minerals including gold**, platinum, pyrite, placer diamonds, silver, uranium, malachite, palladium, sperrylite, and copper in that area.

However, of most interest to me was the mention that Ute Indians described several ancient mining prospects there. Citing an unpublished 1909 firsthand report by J. H. Mullison for the forest atlas, *Medicine Bow National Forest: Geological Survey of Wyoming*, Hausel stated:

> A 67-foot deep shaft sunk in 1886 intersected some older mine workings that contained a tunnel and a 4-foot diameter shaft. The workings were in very poor condition, but before leaving, Mullison found an artifact of a face carved in 'elk's ivory' on the floor of the mine.[35]

The coordinates given for that mine placed it next to Medicine Bow Peak.

Hausel continued concerning another site:

> In the same locality Mullison described an old stone wall along the creek, built to keep the steep bank from caving. Five separate prospects were found near the wall. A short distance from these prospects, Mullison found a 6-foot diameter circular shaft….Trees growing on top of the mine tailings were estimated to be more than 175 years old….[36] [Tailings are the waste discarded in mining after valuable minerals are extracted.]

Later through a series of phone calls I traced down the file for the original 1909 report of Mullison. I would have liked more firsthand details or to have known what the face on the elk's ivory looked like. Eventually the report was located, but mysteriously the part about the small shafts and the carving of the face, though also quoted in other sources, is now missing.

Today mines in America are mammoth caverns beneath the ground with room for heavy equipment. The mines mentioned by Mullison with only four or six foot shafts, had to have been used by people very small in stature.

Numerous reports tell that most Native Americans before the arrival of Caucasians were not interested in gold. Because there was no other explanation for those mines, it was rumored that they were dug by Spaniards. However, historians scoff at that explanation because there is no reliable report that Spaniards got that far north that early. Reportedly the first Caucasians reached the area of Medicine Bow Peak in 1817.[37]

The mines and stone workmanship of the McKean Complex people in Wyoming were especially noteworthy. The area of their rock work encompassed 400 to 600 square miles and is thought to have been done without metal tools. The mines included both pits and tunnels. That rock work stretched from a few miles northeast of Medicine Bow Peak to Manville. Basically it followed the tributaries of the Laramie and North Platte Rivers to their junction.

History of Wyoming states:

> Arrow and lance heads and hide scrapers are found beautifully fashioned from brilliantly colored agates, jasper and chalcedony. All colors are represented, white, blue, red, yellow, black and banded. Work on these is… superior….Indians of today….have no knowledge of the system of mining these huge quarries.[38]

> In no section of the entire world can be found ancient quarries of such magnitude….[There were] pits, tunnels, open cuts and immense bodies of rock dumps….the region was suddenly abandoned….tons of cores left just in the beginning of being shaped.[39]

Early Chinese also mined. According to UNESCO, the earliest mining site so far discovered in China contains both pit and underground copper mines. Mining at that site started 3300 years ago and continued through the early Warring States period using booms, pulleys, and wooden props.[40]

West of Laramie we visited the awesome Vedauwoo (pronounced VEE-dah-voo) rock formations. Vedauwoo means "earthborn spirits" in the Native American language of Arapaho and they regarded this location as sacred.

Vedauwoo consists of enormous boulders piled on top of each other. Reportedly they were sculpted by wind and water. They are so large that one has to surmise that surely they are just natural occurrences. However, it seems strange that so many are grouped together in one location.

3 – Medicine Bow Peak, Wyoming

With imagination on the part of the viewer, they form recognizable figures including those which have been named Seal, Bison, Loaf of Bread, Dinosaur Bone, and a precariously balanced Cube. I could envision some of these. My husband just enjoyed them as interesting boulders.

We only skirted Cheyenne, the capitol of Wyoming, but miles away we could see the 24 carat gold gilded capitol dome which shone in the afternoon sun like a beacon. We spent the night in Loveland, Colorado.

4 – Longs Peak, Colorado

And it says that, three hundred li to the south, **KEUCH-WANG Mountain (or Aspen Mountain)** is to be found. Upon this there are **many gems and much gold**, and below it many **green jade-stones**. Wild animals are found there which look like **dogs with six legs**. These are called TS'UNG-TS'UNG, the name being given them in imitation of their cry. **Birds** are also found there which look like domestic fowls, but **which have hair like a rat**. These are called TSZ' rats. When they are seen, the country is subject to great drought. The **CHI River is found here, a stream flowing northerly into HU River**. In this there are many **lancet-fish**. These are of a dark color, spotted (or striped) with blue, and have a bill like a lancet. [These were originally found in the Eastern Sea, and they are now found in the KIANG-TUNG River also.] Those who eat them are not subject to epidemic diseases. (Vining translation of *Shan Hai Jing*)

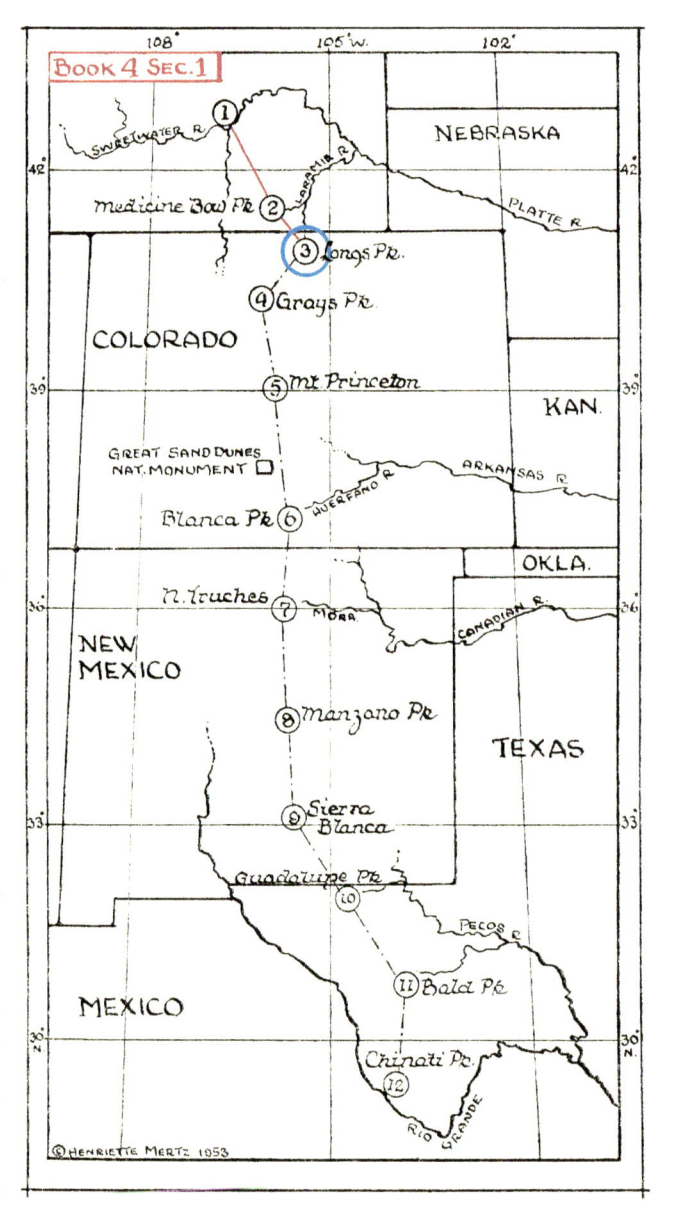

Mertz Note:

> One hundred miles south, "Aspen Mountain" probably is Long's Peak, Colorado. Mile after mile of the most spectacular golden-leafed Aspen trees stretch clear across Colorado – truly an unforgettable sight, even to

4 – Longs Peak, Colorado

the Chinese. Gold, as is well known, abounds in this area from Steamboat Springs to Cripple Creek; [mottled green jade, such as is known in Mexico, comes from this region.][41] The CHI River is a fork of the Laramie which flows north. The two rivers, one from Medicine Bow and the other from Long's Peak, join – as the Chinese noted. Identification of the fish, rainbow or speckled trout or any other, will be left to the fishermen of Colorado. The birds with hair like a rat, may be bats.

Author's Comments:

Here the Chinese account mentions the **Hu River,** which we previously identified at Medicine Bow Peak as the Laramie River. Tracing the Laramie to its source takes us right to the mountains on which Longs Peak sits!

Today the Laramie River starts at Longdraw reservoir. However, before the reservoir was built, the Laramie would have still started there. This is at the northern end of the Front Range in north central Colorado.[42]

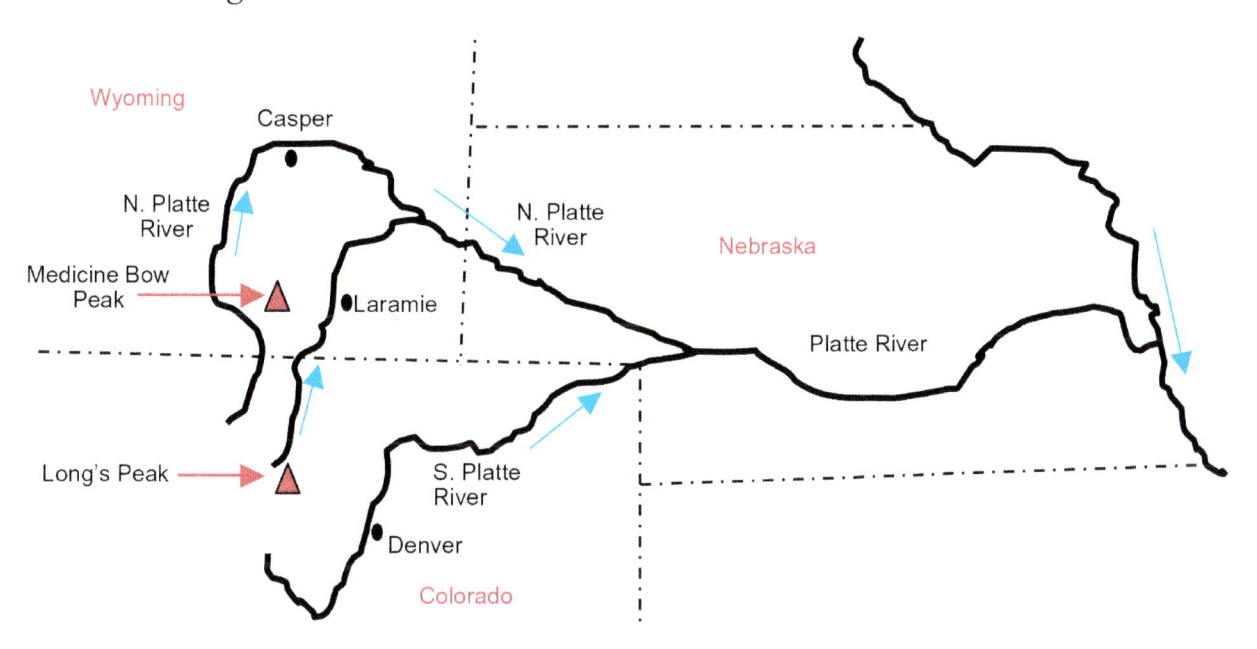

There is a gulch on the western side of Longs Peak. The **CHI River** could very well be this gulch which runs north-south. Since the Laramie River starts at the end of the mountains it is only logical that streams flow down from the mountains to form the headwaters.

Therefore, to arrive at Longs Peak it appears that the Chinese followed the Laramie south from the area near Medicine Bow Peak to its source. To the west of the Laramie River are the headwaters of the North Platte. To the south and east, cradling this area, is the north flowing South Platte River. From there the Laramie flows north until many miles later it joins the North Platte. North and South Platte rivers intersect in Nebraska where the name changes to simply "Platte River."

Around 2006 Dr. H. Mike Xu, who was educated in China and America, sent me a tracing of a petroglyph (rock carving) that he had seen in Colorado that he believed was pre-1800 BC Chinese writing. Previously Dr. Xu published both a book and an article in an academic journal in which he identified writing from celts in Mexico as Chinese of that same period.[43] This area of Colorado is also the vicinity of where the Granby Stone, with its pre-1800 BC Chinese writing, was found.

The Continental Divide Trail, which we encountered at each location so far, does not cross Longs Peak but comes very close at Grand Lake.

Tom's Baby

On the day we flew into that area we had visited Denver Museum of Natural History to view their awesome display of minerals found in Colorado. It highlighted "Tom's Baby," the largest piece of gold ever found in Colorado (156 troy ounces or 13 pounds). On July 23, 1887, Tom Groves walked into Breckenridge, Colorado cradling in his arms the huge nugget wrapped in a blanket. Thus it was named "Tom's Baby."

4 – Longs Peak, Colorado

Principal Gold-Producing Districts of the United States list six locations for **gold** in Boulder County Colorado where Longs Peak is found.[44] One location near Longs Peak is Eugenia Mine, a gold mine which operated for about 12 years starting in 1905. The mine appears to have been somewhat successful in that they used heavy equipment and went 1000 feet deep.

There was lot of opposition to Eugenia Mine from naturalist neighbors. Rocky Mountain National Park bill was signed in 1915. Mining was allowed to continue, but soon the mine was abandoned. Gold is still found at numerous other sites across Colorado.

In conflict with Mertz' statement above, **jade** was not among the minerals the Denver museum displayed for Colorado. A curator suggested that there were other green minerals in Colorado which one might mistake for jade. The region just north of Longs Peak has more than 70 minerals, including numerous gems. The internet displays green amazonite as "Colorado Jade." Wyoming, which boasts jade as their state gem, is only 50 miles away from Longs Peak. It is feasible that jade might have been found at this location at one time.

Dusky Grouse
Note the feathery legs
Photo courtesy of Oregon
Department of Fish and Wildlife

I believe that the *Shan Hai Jing's* mention of a **bird with hair** is the identification of another animal native to North America. Mertz thought the Chinese were describing bats. The Rocky Mountain National Park does list bats among the animals living there. However, the Chinese of that era would have known the difference between bats and birds. Chinese revere bats. For ages Chinese have depicted bats in art and regard bats as omens of good fortune.

The *Shan Hai Jing* stated that the birds here looked like domesticated fowl, surely a reference to chickens, which according to Chinese archeology they had bred by 2000 BC.[45] The English name for these birds, dusky grouse (Dendragapus obscurus), was recently changed from blue grouse. Until now it was believed that the first literary mention of them was by Lewis & Clark in the early 1800s. They are native to the Rocky Mountains of North America and are about the size and shape of chickens. In the colder months they grow downy hair-like feathers (which some have referred to as hair) on their legs and feet. In fact, at a glance the down on gray "hairy" legs of dusky grouse looks similar to fur of mice.

It is difficult to know what type of **fish** they were discussing. Perhaps it was another American species. Colorado pikeminnow, have a bluish cast and a long beak-like snout. Now endangered, pikeminnow can grow to nearly 6 feet long. Another possible candidate for this fish is the razorback sucker which is also native to that area and endangered. That fish has an elongated head which is small in proportion to its body. However, whether these fish have healing properties has not yet been discovered in recent times.

On another one of the *Shan Hai Jing* journeys it was mentioned that by eating a certain fish one could help prevent swelling. Because of the location, which Mertz placed as the Columbia River, she thought it was a reference to salmon. Recently in the 21st century it was discovered that Omega 3 in salmon does indeed help prevent swelling.

I am puzzled by what the **dog with six legs** could possibly be. When I checked with an expert in China to re-translate this, he said that this was "a holy beast that looks like a dog with six legs."

Most people snicker when they hear this description. However, there are anomalies in nature as when twins are conjoined. A few years back a calf in my area of Virginia was born with six legs. However, that is certainly not the norm.

When I was a child and my family was back in the US and living in Indiana, a Chinese man from Taiwan visited. He asked to cook and was shocked when the very first egg he opened had a double yolk. He immediately asked whether all eggs in America had double yolks. Perhaps that was the case with the six-legged dog.

However, perhaps the reference to this six-legged creature was an idiom or had a figurative meaning. One might say in English, "The wolf is at the door," (meaning threat of poverty) and not expect anyone to look for a real wolf.

4 – Longs Peak, Colorado

In Chinese mythology there was a creature representing chaos which was variously named Konton, Dijiang, or Hudun. It was described as a divine dog or a large beast with six legs, four wings, and no head or eyes.

In *A Chinese Bestiary: Strange Creatures from the Guideways Through Mountains and Seas* by University of California Press, Richard E. Strassberg discusses a six-legged Hudun which he also refers to as Dijiang. Strassberg quotes from *Master Zhang* regarding this beast then explains its figurative meaning:

> Here Hudun can be read as a figure of primordial chaos who is a victim of purposeful activity, destroyed by the well-intentioned though dangerously misguided efforts of humanizing civilization.[46]

Therefore, the figurative meaning of the six-legged beast for the *Shan Hai Jing* travelers could have been that the area by Longs Peak was wild and chaotic but that the Chinese were bringing civilization and order.

From Loveland, Colorado we journeyed to Estes Park to enter Rocky Mountain National Park and to see Longs Peak. Traveling up Route 34 we were awed by the beauty of the glistening cliffs and the beautiful yellow aspen as we ascended Big Thompson Canyon Road. We could understand why the Chinese might have named this **Aspen Mountain.**

Estes Park, elevation 7522 feet, lies in the valley below Longs Peak. We had read that in the fall elk congregated in town for the mating season. At the visitor's center we learned that in fact elk were gathered nearby so hurried off to find them.

Longs Peak Courtesy of NPS

- 35 -

In total we saw 14 huge elk. They were near a pond and on a golf course. One enormous elk with huge antlers lay in the grass no more than 15 feet from where we walked by. The golf course had fenced off certain areas to keep the greens from being destroyed. We saw no one playing nor could they even if they wanted to challenge the elk for that turf. A male elk would bugle and another male across the lake would bugle back.

There are lots of little shops in Estes Park and we did a quick run through of several before going on our way again. We had hoped to take the tram up that day for a view of Longs Peak, but the tram was closed. We had also hoped to get a good view of Longs Peak on the day we flew into Denver, but because of recent forest fires in Colorado the skies were hazy then and the view obscured.

Travel books suggested that another way to get a view of Longs Peak was to journey up Trail Ridge Road toward Grand Lake and look back, so we did that. With a scenic highway designation, this is the highest continuously paved highway in the United States.

When we were there it was the weekend. The road was crowded and very winding – sometimes with sheer drop offs and no guard rail. We stopped several times to enjoy the beauty. At one stop, tiny ground squirrels raced out toward us. When we did not feed them, looking for food, they ran over the hands and fingers of others. It is illegal to feed wild animals in the park because they need to learn to be self sufficient. However, apparently some before us had fed them.

Longs Peak at 14,255 feet is the sixteenth tallest of 54 mountains over 14,000 feet high in Colorado. It has a unique flat-topped profile. For most of the year, climbing Longs Peak is in winter conditions which require specialized gear. Hikers accidentally die there almost every year, partly because of the sheer cliffs. Hiking any of the high peaks, one also needs to be alert to altitude sickness which is brought on by lack of oxygen and failure to acclimate. Symptoms include headache, shortness of breath, tightness in the chest, marked fatigue and weakness.

5 – Grays Peak, Colorado

And it says that, three hundred li to the south, PUH T'SAN Mountain is found. It has **no grass or trees, and no water.** (Vining translation of *Shan Hai Jing*)

Mertz Note:

> Of the four or five major peaks approximately 100 miles south, Grays Peak appears to be the one noted by the Chinese.

Author's note:

Grays Peak is as described. There is **no water on the mountain** itself, but at the trailhead as we approached the mountain there was a creek. South Platte River is further south then east of here as it flows north. The Continental Divide Trail, which we have mentioned at every stop so far on this *Shan Hai Jing* journey, goes right over the top of the twin peaks, Torreys and Grays. Grays is the highest peak on the Continental Divide Trail.[47]

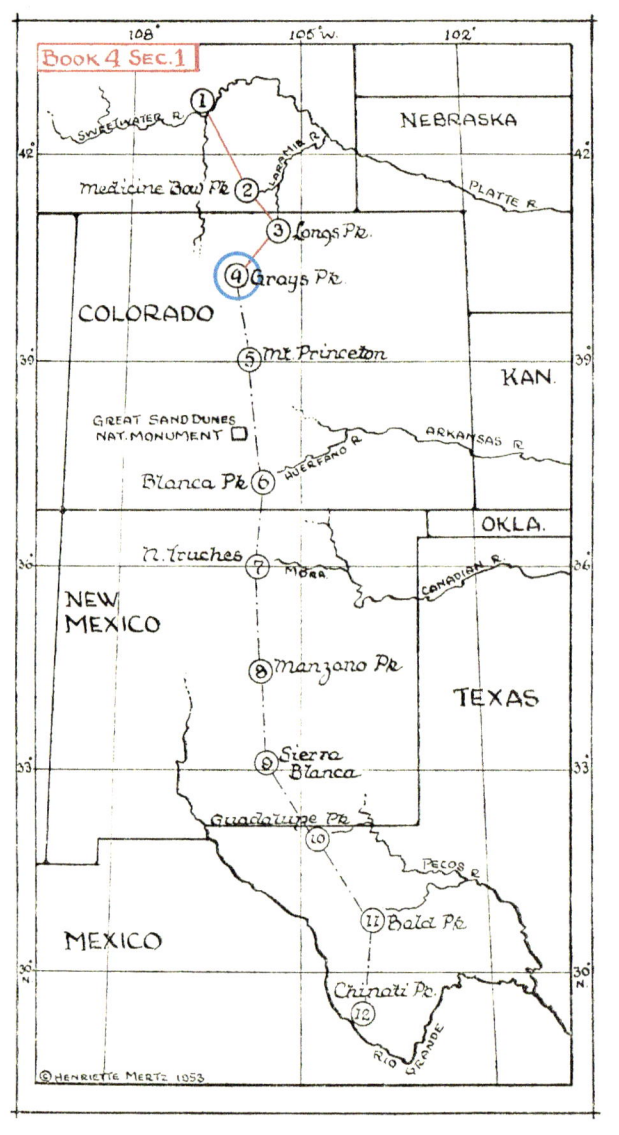

From Estes Park near Longs Peak, we traveled to Dillon, Colorado. That day involved a lot of driving because we went through Estes Park, Grand Lake, Granby, then on to Dillon.

The *Archaeology of Colorado* described unexplained sites with wattle and daub houses near Granby, Colorado. Wattle and daub structures typically are built from a base of woven wooden strips covered by a mixture of wet earth and straw. These were carbon dated to around 4000 years ago – the same time period that some scholars put Chinese there. A nearby jasper quarry was used to make tools. The people, whose stay there seemed brief, were unexplainably more advanced than those before and immediately after them.

> The scanty deposits of tools and discarded foodstuffs are indicative of short-term habitations, as would be expected in an intermountain [sic] valley over 8,000 feet above sea level. This is what has made the presence of substantial structures so puzzling to some.[48]

Could these have been the dwellings of the *Shan Hai Jing* Chinese survey team, whose time there would have been brief? Some Chinese structures of that era were also wattle and daub as these in Colorado were. Travelers always prefer a standard of living similar to what they have at home so it is no surprise that they would build a nice shelter, even if for short term.

Granby is just a few miles west of Longs Peak, our previous stop on this particular *Shan Hai Jing* journey. The McKean Complex was also found at numerous sites in Colorado including Fourth of July Valley, about 15 miles due south of Longs Peak. Fourth of July Valley is southeast of Granby – down a canyon and on a trail connected to Granby Lake. In fact, McKean Complex sites are found at numerous other locations on the *Shan Hai Jing* trail.

Creek at the trailhead to Grays Peak

In *Secret Maps of the Ancient World*[49] I discussed the Granby Stone, found there in 1920 when William Chalmers was scooping a reservoir. The Granby Stone (or Granby Idol as some call it) has writing on it identified as pre-18th century BC Chinese.

I first read about the Granby Stone in Dr. Cyclone Covey's *A Critical Reprise of 'Aboriginal' American History.*[50] Then Dr. Betty Meggers of the Smithsonian gave me photos of it when she came to hear me speak at the Library of Congress in 2005. Several good sets of photos of the stone still exist, but now the 66 pound artifact has disappeared.

Did Ancient Chinese Explore America?

Mastodon (left), Chinese writing (center), dinosaur (right), on Granby Stone

Much was matching up to the Chinese journeys, but in the real world it cannot be exactly 100 miles between every stop. These distances had to have been approximations. Apparently Mertz charted the course on maps with a ruler from one mountain top to another to calculate distances, so they are "as the crow flies." At the end of her text concerning the last stop of this journey she discusses the mystery of how this was calculated by the Chinese.

Today one has to travel where the roads are. Much of this trip is through mountainous areas. There are only a limited number of routes to get to one's next location and those often involve winding highways.

If the Chinese really were there, what system did they use to measure? Some suggested that the Chinese surveyors used counting sticks, but after so far surely those would have been too burdensome. If they were traveling by the rivers, those meander. Even if they were taking the paths now used as the Continental Divide Trail, those are not straight lines either.

Since they knew astronomy, were the Chinese explorers calculating distances by using the stars? *History of Cartography* states:

> Astronomical methods were early used to determine the position of points. Chinese tradition places the first maps in about 2000 BC.[51]

5 – Grays Peak, Colorado

My brother and I discovered in Texas in 2009 on the southern part of this *Shan Hai Jing* trip that from the mountain top the named mountains 100 miles away, both north and south, were visible even on a hazy day. Perhaps the Chinese used that method or perhaps they picked out the highest peaks on the horizon as the next destination. Many questions are still unanswered.

Two photos of Stevens Gulch Road

It was a full day of travel so we were very glad that our hotel in Dillon had a hot tub. The outdoor hot tub felt wonderful in the crisp mountain air. The aspen trees glistened in beautiful shades of gold. This was one location where we scheduled two nights lodging. We used the hot tub both evenings after our daytime travels.

Did Ancient Chinese Explore America?

We had planned to rise at 5:30 the first morning in Dillon in order to be at Grays Peak at sunrise for the best photo shot, but were unsure of the condition of the road to the trailhead. Dave had not been sleeping well at night and when I awoke at 5:28 he was breathing softly. I decided to turn off the alarm before it rang.

Grays Peak & Torreys Peak

Entrance to silver mine and tailings

After a full night's sleep and a nice breakfast provided by the motel, we set out for Grays Peak. We traveled about 20 miles up I-70 to exit 221 Bakersville and took Stevens Gulch Road to the trailhead. Stevens Gulch Road is no longer maintained so ideally one needs a 4 wheel drive vehicle to navigate it.[52] However, Dave managed by driving slowly over four miles of ruts to the end of the road. Weather can change suddenly and in winter that lane is not passable. Most cell phones are inoperable there.

On reaching the trailhead we were surprised to see about 75 cars already there that Saturday morning, but fortunately we found a parking place.

The day was perfect, around 60 degrees Fahrenheit. The sky was clear and blue with little wind. Almost immediately after we started walking we were above the tree line.

From the trail, one can view entrances to the old silver mine across the creek and the valley. We missed the display of wildflowers that fill that basin in July and August.[53]

Tom's Baby, the 13 pound gold nugget previously mentioned, was found only about 15 miles from Grays Peak as the crow flies. The first silver to be discovered in Colorado was at Stevens Gulch. A claim was staked in 1865.

The elevation at the trailhead is 11,270 feet[54] and the peak 14,270.[55] At first the trail seemed easy with wide steps but soon the elevation took its toll. I only planned to go about one mile, high enough to take a good photo where both Grays Peak and Torreys Peak are in full view. That location is over 12,000 feet. However, it seemed farther than the described mile. Perhaps it was two miles each way.

Dave, who at home works out at the YMCA six days a week, had difficulty with nausea and breathing because of the altitude. He told me to go on ahead. Meanwhile, several people passed us coming or going. A young couple walked past talking about a mountain lion they had seen. At 12:30 p.m. I met a man and his dog. They already had been to the top and back since 6 a.m. One man walked down the trail with his baby on his back. These folks had to have been better acclimated to the elevation than we were.

Denver, at 5280 feet elevation, is known as the mile high city. The first day, when we arrived there, I developed a bad headache from the elevation change. Our home in Virginia is around 600 feet elevation, but on Grays Peak we were at around 20 times that! At home I exercise regularly, but it took me an hour to descend from whatever distance I had gone.

Did Ancient Chinese Explore America?

View of Vail from gondola

I was happy to return to the hot tub in Dillon. Dave checked the football scores. The next morning we attended the 9 a.m. service at Rocky Mountain Bible Church in Fresco, a cute little town with the ambience of Switzerland. After that we went to Vail for a few hours. On the way we saw old mine shafts sticking out of the rocks above the highway. In the vicinity are towns named Golden, Silverthorne, Silver Plume, Granite, Copper Hill, Gypsum, Basalt, and Leadville – indicative of their association to mining.

Vail was lovely. By our good fortune it was the last day of gondola rides to the top. As we ascended we saw people riding dirt bikes down the mountain. At the top we took a short walking trail overlooking valleys on both sides. The views were of blue skies, green meadows, and miles and miles of golden aspen trees. A memorial service at the top had just concluded. As we ate lunch in a restaurant at the peak, we listened to a lone bagpiper in the distance.

Later when I learned that there had been a McKean Complex site in the valley by Vail, I smiled to think that those early people must have enjoyed the same beauty, thousands of years ago.

5 – Grays Peak, Colorado

Our trip to our next destination took us down Highway 24 which is very winding. In some places the speed limit is only 20 miles per hour. Train tracks wind through the valley. Even though it was still September, we could already see snow on some of the mountain tops.

View from Highway 24 with train tracks below

In Leadville we stopped to visit the National Mining Hall of Fame and Museum, which was quite informative and much larger than we expected. Leadville was a boom town with the discovery of gold and silver in the late 19th century. At one time it was the second most populous city in Colorado and some claim it was even slated to be capital of Colorado.[56]

Large companies with origins in Leadville include May Company (which later became Macys), Guggenheims, Marshall Fields, W. B. Daniels, and James V. Dexter. Molly Brown arrived in Leadville as a teenager in the 1880s. She was a seamstress who married into wealth and eventually became the "Unsinkable Molly Brown" of Titanic fame. Those who visited the town include Teddy Roosevelt, Texas Jack,

Buffalo Bill, "Chicken Bill" Lovell, "Broken Nose" Scotty, and Soapy Smith.[57] Susan B. Anthony lectured for women's suffrage, John Philip Sousa performed, and Oscar Wilde spoke in Leadville. " 'Doc' Holliday (dentist turned gambler) had his final shootout at Hyman's Saloon."[58]

However, those days are past. The 2010 census for the whole county lists only 7310 residents. Currently Leadville touts: "70 square blocks…designated as a National Historic Landmark District of Victorian architecture"[59] and the Scenic Historic Highway. "It is one of America's last authentic mining towns." At over 10,430 feet it is called "the two mile high city" or "Cloud City."[60]

6 – Mount Princeton, Colorado

And it says that, three hundred li to the south, FAN-T'IAO Mountain (or the Foreign Range) is to be found. It has **no grass or trees, but has much sand**. The KIEN (**Diminishing**) **River** is found here, a stream **flowing northerly** into the sea. In this there are many KAN fish (The **KAN fish** is described as a fish three feet long, that is found in the YANG-TSZ' River, having a large mouth and **yellowish gills, and greenish back**.) [One authority names these "the yellow-jawed fish."] (Vining translation of *Shan Hai Jing*)

Mertz Note:

> Mount Princeton, 100 miles south, immediately north of Monarch Pass, is probably the high peak, with the Sangre de Cristo Range, which starts there, being the "foreign range" mentioned in the record. The Chinese state that they found much sand. Along the western side of the crest of the Sangre de Cristo Range, stretches mile after mile of sand – culminating in our Great Sand Dunes National Monument. Sand there is. The "Diminishing River" is a tributary of the Arkansas.

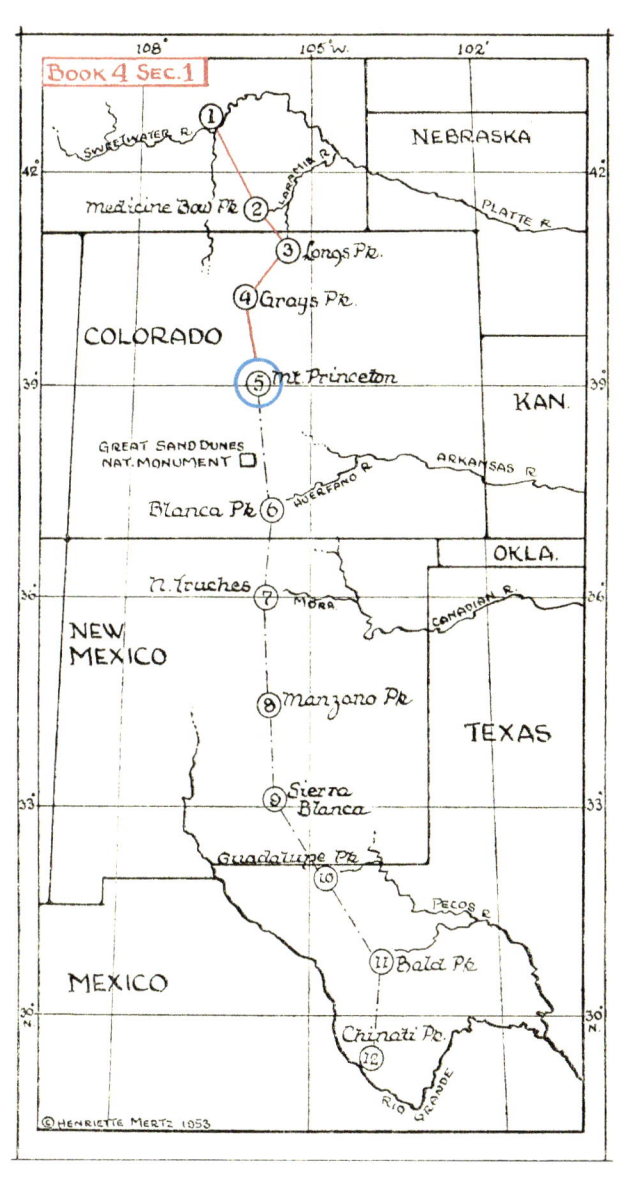

Author's Comments:

Mt. Princeton is as described. It has **no trees and no grass and is somewhat sandy**. As Mertz stated, this area is the beginning of mile after mile of sand culminating in

- 47 -

the Great Sand Dunes National Park, close to our next stop on this *Shan Hai Jing* journey.

The Continental Divide Trail, mentioned at every previous stop on this *Shan Hai Jing* Journey, continues to this area as well. Mt. Princeton is cradled between the north-south bound Continental Divide Trail to the west and the north-south Colorado Trail to the east.

In the vicinity of Mt. Princeton are beautiful towering white chalk cliffs and several 14,000 foot peaks called the Collegiate Mountains. They include Princeton, Harvard, Columbia, Yale, and Oxford. In the next *Shan Hai Jing* journey (Book 4 Section 2) Mertz charted that trip as going to Mt. Harvard.

Creeks, both to the north and south of Mt. Princeton, **run north**east for a few miles until they flow into the south bound Arkansas River.[61] The Arkansas eventually joins the Mississippi River flowing into the Gulf of Mexico. A little to the north of Mt. Princeton the Arkansas and South Platte rivers come very close to each other, but do not intersect. Just east of Buena Vista, Colorado is the divide between the drainage of the Arkansas River and the South Platte.[62]

Mount Princeton photo courtesy of Daniel Zajic

Because of the abundance and variety of local fish, paid fishing trips depart from Buena Vista. The **Kan fish with yellowish gills and green back** mentioned in the *Shan Hai Jing* may be yellowfin cutthroat trout (Oncorhynchus clarki macdonaldi) which were native to America and found at the Twin Lakes at the headwaters of the Arkansas River but are now extinct. These fish grew to weigh over 10 pounds.[63]

> The yellowfin cutthroat trout, first identified in Colorado in 1891, is now presumed extinct. Originally found near the headwaters of Colorado's Arkansas River, the yellowfin cutthroat was wiped out when rainbow trout were introduced into its Twin Lakes home.

> In early reports, the yellowfin cutthroat trout were described as "silvery olive: a broad lemon yellow shade along the sides, lower fins bright golden yellow in life, no red anywhere except the deep red dash on each side of the throat."[64]

There is also a greenback cutthroat trout (Oncorhynchus clarki ssp. stomias) native to this area, but its gills are more orange than yellow. The greenback cutthroat was presumed to be extinct in 1937 but some have since been found.

The writer of the *Shan Hai Jing* said that the fish here were the same species he had seen in the Yang-Tsz' River (China). Both were trout. Brown trout (Salmo trutta) are native to Europe, northern Africa, and Asia. Brown trout, now also found in the rivers of Colorado, are only slightly green on the back. However, reportedly the first brown trout in the US were imported from Germany in 1883. They are not native to North America, but were introduced at various locations across nearly every state.[65] Therefore, the *Shan Hai Jing* writer might have seen a trout before, but perhaps not exactly the same variety.

Travelers always need a nearby source of water. So far on this journey it appears that the Chinese first followed the north branch of the Platte River, then the Laramie to the south branch of the Platte. At this intersection near the Arkansas it seems that they left the South Platte, but continued south following the Arkansas for a short way.

Lest one thinks that is a wild supposition, years later in 1820, President James Madison sent Major Stephen H. Long of the US Army Engineers to lead a scientific exploration of the Platte River. The account tells that after covering both branches of the river and naming Longs Peak and the Rockies, Long and his men went down the South Platte to this same Arkansas watershed.[66]

Dave and I had read about a popular lodge with a hot spring near Mt. Princeton so delayed our arrival to when there was a vacancy. This location had served as a stop for stagecoaches starting in 1850, then as a stop on the Denver South Park and Pacific Railroad in the late 19th century. We read that visitors then and now enjoy the healing waters of the hot springs which come up in the sandy bottomed creek.[67]

On arriving I immediately wanted to try the hot springs. We were told that next to the bank of the creek the hot water comes out at 135 degrees Fahrenheit (57 Celsius). The object is to find a sandy depression part way out into the stream, where the cold creek water and the hot spring water mix to a comfortable temperature, and then lie down there.

Map of Stephen H. Long

We did not have water shoes and our first adventure was trying to climb down the huge boulders on the creek bank which had no hand rail. After descending the hill, I stepped into the scalding water at the edge of the stream. Immediately, in order to escape the heat, I tried to maneuver around others to a cooler location. Fortunately for me, some children seeing my distress and floundering motions, abandoned their spot in the creek.

I was just getting comfortable when I turned to watch my husband descend the bank like a large bear. His feet are even more sensitive than mine. As soon as his feet were in the water I heard a yell then saw him attempt to scramble back up the boulders. I watched in both amusement and horror, fearing that he would fall and break a leg. We decided to retreat to the heated swimming pool and then later to a regular hot tub elsewhere on the property. Perhaps our days of dashing and splashing in creek beds are over.

We purposely chose to stay at the hot springs because we read in a travel book that we would wake up to views of Mt. Princeton and so paid extra for a room with that panorama. The chalk cliffs there are beautiful, but a tree which had grown up was blocking the vista from the large window at the back of our room. If we had been one room over, perhaps it would have been better.

Then we learned that what we might have seen, had the tree not been there, was not Mt. Princeton at all. To see Mt. Princeton we had to walk out the front door, across the parking lot, crane our necks, and then we could only see part of the peak.

Daniel Zajic and his sister, who had just hiked to the top to Mt. Princeton and back that day, were staying in a room near ours. I quizzed them at length about what the top of the mountain was like. They reported a lot of loose rock and **sand** at the top, just like the *Shan Hai Jing* stated.

Daniel Zajic at top of Mt. Princeton 23 September 2012
(Photo courtesy of Daniel Zajic)

Daniel said that we would have to drive a few miles to Buena Vista in the morning to get a good distance shot of Mt. Princeton.

We rose before daylight to be at the right location as the sun came up. Sipping coffee and stale breakfast biscuits from a gas station (instead of the sumptuous breakfast we could have enjoyed at the resort), we sat waiting in silence for dawn.

Did Ancient Chinese Explore America?

It snowed during the night on the mountain tops. Potentially our photos should have been good, but the morning was misty. Fortunately, Daniel Zajic sent me his photos of the peak, which he took the previous day. If they had hiked one day later, Daniel and his sister would have been blocked by ice and snow from reaching the summit.

After attempting to take a few shots of Mt. Princeton we headed back toward the resort, but then decided that since we were already up we should go in the early dawn hours to see St. Elmo, a nearby ghost town. It is said to be one of the most preserved ghost towns in Colorado.[68]

St. Elmo used to be a mining town and is down a well maintained and tree lined dirt road. At some locations a gurgling stream runs beside the lane. On the way deer crossed in front of us a couple of times. Dave was driving and I am not a good photographer. Both times I fumbled with the camera and missed the best shots of the deer.

6 – Mount Princeton, Colorado

The ghost town was no disappointment. Lace curtains are still in windows of some on the deserted and dilapidated houses. We saw lights on at one place, so apparently one house in that town is still occupied – by someone or something.

Back at the resort we decided to try the hot tub, not the creek, for one last time before checking out. Soon after we left the lodge to head for our next destination six large elk crossed the road. Again I fumbled with the camera and missed the shot while yelling in excitement and frustration, "Oh! Oh! Oh! Oh!" My ever patient husband calmly drove on.

7 – Blanca Peak, Colorado

And it says that, four hundred li to the south, KU-MAO Mountain (or **Mountain of the Maiden**) is found. Upon this there are many **lacquer-trees**, and below it many **mulberry-trees**, and **silk-worm oaks**. KU-MAO River is found here, a **stream flowing northerly into the sea**, in which there are many **KAN fish**. (Vining translation of *Shan Hai Jing*)

Mertz note:

> Blanca, the "White Maiden," Spanish name for the Chinese identification of the "Mountain of the Maiden," stands 130 miles due south. The Huerfano, a tributary of the Arkansas, flows northerly from Blanca Peak to join the Arkansas.

Author's Comments:

Our next stop after Mt. Princeton was Blanca Peak. In Spanish "blanca" can mean either "white" or "white woman." Therefore, perhaps Mertz was correct in saying that **Mountain of the Maiden** is similar in meaning.

When viewing Blanca Peak from two miles out on Google Maps, the shadows on the southern side of that mountain create an illusion of a woman's face. (Even my husband can see it!) However, while in that area and viewing Blanca Peak, we did not

- 54 -

notice that. If Mertz is correct and both the Chinese and the early Spaniards named this mountain in reference to a woman, perhaps that illusion is visible from land at certain times of day.

Mertz was also correct in saying that the **Huerfano flows north from Blanca Peak** to join the Arkansas. About halfway between Mt. Princeton and Blanca Peak the Arkansas River turns almost due east until it meets the Mississippi, which flows south to the Gulf of Mexico.

Blanca Peak

Blanca Peak at 14,345 feet is the highest mountain on this *Shan Hai Jing* journey. It is in the Sangre de Cristo Range, a sub group of the Rocky Mountains which extends from Colorado down into New Mexico.

Sangre de Cristo translates from Spanish as "the blood of Christ." According to legend, this name was given to the mountains by a wounded and dying Catholic priest when he saw the mountains colored a fiery red by a beautiful sunset.

Blanca Peak was one of the Navajo Indians' four sacred mountains. This area was previously part of Nuevo Mexico Province, Mexico, but in 1848 was sold to the United States under the treaty of Guadalupe Hidalgo. Here in the valley is Colorado's oldest town, San Luis. The legendary "Kit" Carson commanded a fortress nearby.

The *Shan Hai Jing* said that there were **mulberry trees** in this location and sure enough, unexplainably they are there. According to the US Department of Agriculture, they are found in a band spreading east starting in Las Animas County, Colorado, which is less than 5 miles from Blanca. However, these are not just any mulberry trees. They are wild white mulberry (morus alba), a species not native to America, but native to China.

According to *World Trade and Biological Exchanges Before 1492*, plants of this species were in the New World before the arrival of Europeans. That book cited the writings of a Catholic priest who died in 1522. He stated that upon his arrival to the Antilles there were "as many mulberries as weeds" already growing there.[69]

Mulberry trees were very important to the Chinese. Starting before 2000 BC in China, silk was made from the cocoons of silk worms fed on mulberry leaves. At early dates the bark from mulberry trees was also used to make bark cloth and/or paper such as the fine paper on which my father's map collection is found.

I remember mulberry trees from my childhood in Taiwan. When I was about eight years old I bought some silk worms, faithfully fed them mulberry leaves, and they spun cocoons. In my youthful zeal I did not realize that the next steps were complicated and that I did not know the process to make silk.

According to the *Shan Hai Jing* account above, this area also had **oak** leaves that another variety of Chinese silk worms ate. Rocky Mountain White Oak (quercus gambelii) is native to this area. Although they are native to China, the moths of Chinese silk worms (antheraea pernyi) that eat oak leaves, including those of white oak, are listed among the wild moths currently in North America.

The *Shan Hai Jing* also mentioned **lacquer trees** (toxicondendron vernicifluum) in this location, but we could not find evidence of them anywhere in the United States. They were formerly known as rhus vernicifluа, and are native to East Asia. Like poison ivy, these trees frequently cause allergic reactions in humans. If lacquer trees ever were in Colorado, perhaps they were later eradicated.

When I inquired about lacquer trees, the ranger at the Great Sand Dunes National Park stated that rabbitbrush (Ericameria nauseosa) grows wild in the area and was used during WWII to make rubber. He surmised that rabbitbrush might be used as a lacquer and he was right. Rubber is currently used as a varnish in some nail finishes.

The **KAN fish**, mentioned previously at Mt. Princeton and now here, must be a general reference to trout. *Travel Colorado* lists the fish types of the Huerfano River as Brook Trout, Cutthroat Trout, and Rainbow Trout.[70] Cutthroat is the only one of these native to Colorado.[71] When non-native fish were introduced, they eradicated some species of indigenous fish.[72]

7 – Blanca Peak, Colorado

To get to Blanca Peak and the Great Sand Dunes National Park from Mt. Princeton we drove down the San Luis Valley, an extremely flat area. The valley lies between two mountain ranges boasting many peaks, ten of which are over 14,000 feet high. It is sandy, as the Chinese description for Mt. Princeton said it would be.

Dave, who was raised in Illinois, which is also very flat, commented: "This is the straightest and flattest road I have ever driven."

The ground is composed of a deep layer of sand, gravel, and sediment with occasional scrub brush or grass on the surface. We saw bulldozers scooping up sand for transport. The valley stretches from 20 to 50 miles wide and about 100 miles from north to south.

At approximately 7500 feet elevation, this is the highest valley in the world capable of sustaining agriculture. There is some irrigation. In most of the valley depth to ground water is only 12 feet.

Studies indicate that there were extensive prehistoric water distribution systems in parts of the American Southwest. The San Luis Valley Community Wetlands Strategy states:

> Records from some of the Spanish expeditions into the Valley report irrigation was used by… indigenous peoples for agriculture.[73]

Mark Guthrie wrote *Colorado Mountains Prehistoric Context* (which included the San Luis Valley) for the Colorado Historical Society. In that report he mentioned two archeological sites which included both lithic scatter and water control.[74] The presence of the lithic scatter (chips of stone implements) suggests that the water control started very early.

The earliest Spanish settlers to San Luis and Conejos continued the use of irrigation ditches for crops. Spanish settlers came up trails following the Rio Grande from Santa Fe, New Mexico, which incidentally is near our next *Shan Hai Jing* stop.

Men hunted in the San Luis valley at very early dates. Large stone spear and dart points were found here close to remains of prehistoric buffalo.

At first I was perplexed that although the Chinese mentioned sand starting at Mt. Princeton, they do not refer to the sand dunes, which are an obvious feature of this area. However, according to the National Park Service the sand dunes were not always there. At one time there was a large lake in the center of the valley. Later the valley had to have had a lot of vegetation to support the large animals that lived there. One might guess that the Chinese arrived after the disappearance of the large animals and before the sand dunes.

To the north of the San Luis Valley, the Continental Divide Trail moves to the mountains on the western side. Blanca Peak is to the east. There are old trails on both sides of the valley.

The trace to the east side of the valley where we find Blanca Peak, the town of Blanca, and the sand dunes is "Los Caminos Antiguos," which translates from Spanish: "the way of the ancient ones."

Today Los Caminos Antiguos lies beneath modern highways. The section of Los Caminos Antiguos here in the San Luis Valley is listed in National Geographic's "Drives of a Lifetime Series"[75] and also in "Scenic Drives USA."[76] It was an old trail even when the Spanish arrived. From Colorado it goes south into New Mexico.

From early dates Native Americans traveled and traded great distances. There are shells from the California coast even in graves that date to archaic times. The trail system spread out throughout the entire southwest United States.[77]

While visiting the San Luis Valley we stayed at the Ramada Inn in Alamosa because of its proximity to Blanca Peak. This inn is economical and sports a nice restaurant and indoor water park with a huge slide available to overnight guests.

The Rio Grande, which originates in Colorado, flows through Alamosa. This and the next several stops of the *Shan Hai Jing Journey*, as charted by Mertz, are in the Rio Grande vicinity.

The City of Alamosa calls itself the "Land of Cool Sunshine." The official visitor's guide credits this valley with 320 days of sunshine each year. The *Alamosa Community Guide* stated:

> Not including partly sunny or partly cloudy days, Alamosa has 148 days a year of full sun….In Alamosa, the daytime summer temperatures average around 80 degrees and can sometimes fall during the night as much as 35-40 degrees…very few homes have air conditioning.[78]

The average annual temperature is 41.1 F. and the average max temperature 58.8 F. Annual precipitation is only 7.25 inches. However, on summer afternoons the sand on the dunes can reach 150 degrees F (66 C).[79]

The Great Sand Dunes National Park is not far from Alamosa and has many species of animals. There one may encounter bears or mountain lions. A nature conservancy which raises bison is on the road to and not far from the sand dunes. For a fee one can stay at that conservancy or by appointment take a two hour tour.

Dust storm approaching Blanca Peak

We arrived in Alamosa around noon. The weather was clear and sunny. About an hour later a storm suddenly came up. As we drove to the sand dunes, the sky behind us grew pitch black with blowing sand. Dirt devils and tumble weeds danced in the road ahead. Almost as quickly as it started, the sand storm passed, followed by hard rain with lightning, then a drizzle.

The Great Sand Dunes encompass 30 square miles and are the tallest dunes in North America. At the visitor center we viewed sand particles under a microscope. The particles sparkled like jewels of many colors. Displays indicated that at one time some people wanted to mine the dunes for the small amount of gold found in them. However, conservationists prevailed.

The exhibit includes mammoth bones and a fish fossil found there. We were told that the presence of that fish fossil suggests that at one time the area was under at least 15 feet of water.

Did Ancient Chinese Explore America?

The Visitor Center warns about dangers of frequent lightning strikes. We returned to walk on the dunes the next day and were told that rain was expected again that second afternoon, so it was safest to walk on the dunes in the morning. During the night rain dampened the sand making our walk easier. Going out onto the dunes was awe inspiring. Following the peak of the ridges was the easiest way.

Great Sand Dunes National Park

In the spring of the year visitors to the dunes play in a creek with pulsating waves. The water is from snow melt from nearby mountains. When we were there, we saw rocks of various colors, including green and red, in the then dry creek bed. From the dunes we saw snow on the highest mountain peaks.

At the edge of the dunes a park ranger gave an interesting demonstration of several objects found there and also about animals living in that location now or in the past. He passed around a camel tooth, a mammoth tooth, and an arrowhead found in the area. Man and mammoth co-existed there at one time. When asked how long ago that was, he said: "Some say it was as recently as 4000 years ago."

7 – Blanca Peak, Colorado

The park ranger mentioned that just a few days earlier a mountain lion came down over the dunes. There are no rattlesnakes or scorpions in this area. At night several small animals including kangaroo rats come out. These are small like mice, but can jump four feet high. Coyotes and elk wander through. Indian rice grass, blowout grass, and scurfpea grow in marshy depressions between the dunes.[80]

The tiny speck to the right in the photo is a person

- 61 -

We visited nearby Zapata Falls. It involved about a three mile drive up a dirt/gravel road then a half mile hike. I thought I saw petroglyphs high on a cliff as we approached the falls.

Near Zapata Falls

There were numerous locations on this *Shan Hai Jing* journey where I thought that perhaps I saw petroglyphs. At another location I sought out a park ranger to ask whether that was what I had seen. The reluctant reply was that they were there, but that they were supposed to be a secret.

Documented and undocumented petroglyphs are at many sites across the western United States. They need to be considered by experts who are open to the concept of transpacific travel at early dates.

We thought that the best viewing area of Blanca Peak was on the highway outside the town of Blanca. After spending several hours that day in Great Sand Dunes National Park we drove to our next stop where we had reserved a room at Rancho de Chimayo, a bed and breakfast not far from Santa Fe, New Mexico.

As we left the area of Blanca Peak we wondered whether it was coincidence that the previously mentioned trail, Los Caminos Antiguos, "the way of the ancient ones," goes through Las Animas County near Blanca. This is not only where the wild white mulberry trees native to China are found, but also where San Luis, which boasted irrigation from before the arrival of the Spaniards, also stands.

8 – North Truchas Peak, New Mexico

And it says that, four hundred li to the south, KAO-SHI Mountain is to be found. Upon this there are **many gems** and below it **many sharp stones**. [From these they are able to make smooth lancets to cure boils and swellings.] CHU-SHING River is found here, **a stream flowing easterly into a marsh**, and in it there are **many gems and much gold**. (Vining translation of *Shan Hai Jing*)

Mertz note:

North Truches (sic) Peak, highest point in New Mexico, appears to be the peak identified in the Classics. There are two streams flowing easterly from the peak that appear to be surrounded with marsh, both are shown interrupted. Semi-precious stones of many kinds are found in the territory – turquoise is there in abundance, as is rock-crystal and jadeite.

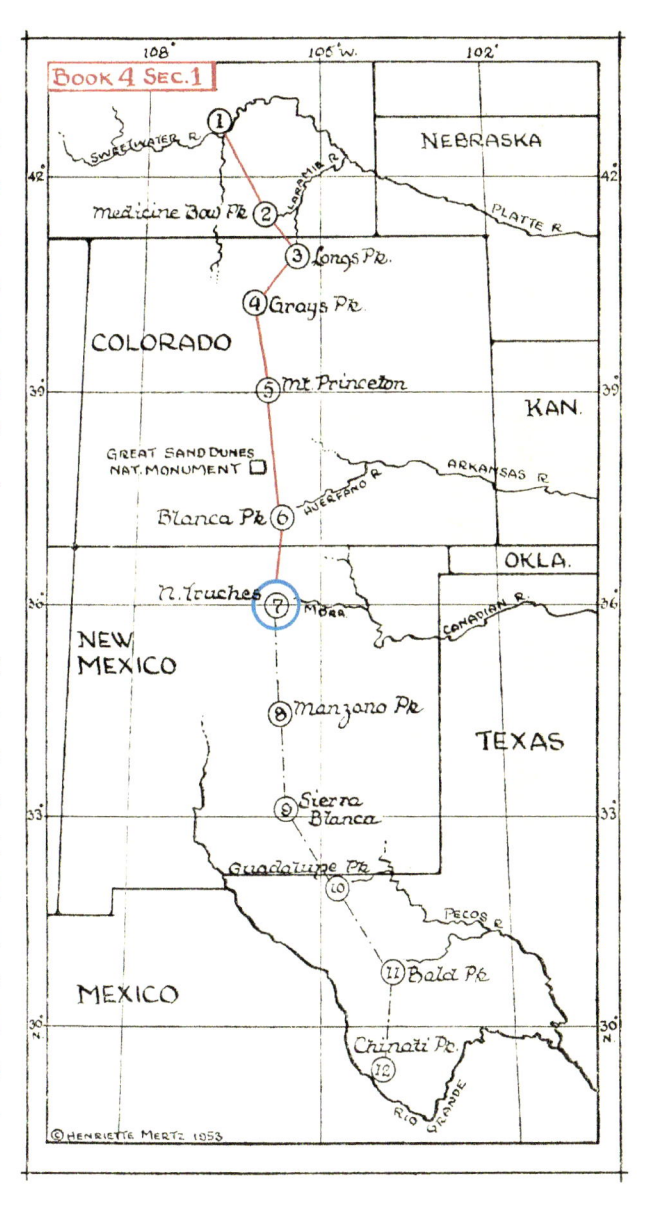

Author's Comments:

Maps indicate that there are **streams that descend from the eastern side** of the Truchas mountains, but they seem to disappear and do not flow into any river.

"New Mexico Gold Map" on Gold Maps Online indicates that there are currently 16,499 active gold mining claims in New Mexico. **Gold and other gems** have been found in several locations in the county surrounding North Truchas Peak.

It appears that copper and pegmatite (which can contain aquamarine, topaz, and other gems) were separately mined at several sites in the county at early dates. It is assumed that this early mining was done by the Spanish, but there are no mining records from that period.[81] There is also evidence of early mining of chert and obsidian, which is credited to the Native Americans.

The Rio Grande River runs through the valley west of North Truchas Peak. Like our last *Shan Hai Jing* stop (Blanca Peak), North Truchas Peak is also in the Sangre de Cristo Range. The Sangre de Cristo Range is considered part of the Rocky Mountains. Mt. Princeton, the stop before Blanca Peak, was just north of but near where the Sangre de Cristo Range started.

We spent the night at historic Rancho de Chimayo, which has both a nice restaurant and bed and breakfast. It was reasonably priced and a very good choice.

Courtyard at Rancho de Chimayo

As we drove out from Santa Fe to Rancho de Chimayo, it seemed a long distance of winding road. Since this is family owned and thus not a chain we knew, we were not sure what we would be facing. When we pulled up, we saw that a huge tour bus had brought its patrons to the restaurant. The meal was delicious, using locally grown chili peppers for which the area is known.

The room where we slept had a fireplace which they offered to light, but Dave felt it was too warm for that. In the morning we were served breakfast on a flower lined patio outside our room at our chosen time.

That part of northern New Mexico became increasingly settled by Spanish after 1692. In 1693 Jose Jaramillo Negrete moved to New Mexico from Mexico along with his wife and an adult son, a Spanish soldier. In the early 1700s Jose's grandson acquired property in Chimayo where the family spread out. In the 1800s two great, great, great grandsons of Jose built their homes where the restaurant and bed and breakfast stand today. That property is still owned by family. In 1965 one brother's restored adobe walled home became the restaurant. In 1984 the other brother's restored home across the road opened as the hacienda.

Truchas Mountains in 2008 by Jerry Friedman

North Truchas at 13,024 feet is the sixth highest peak in New Mexico. It can be viewed well from the town of Truchas, only a short distance up the road from where we stayed in Chimayo. On the evening that we arrived it was raining so that was not a good time to photograph the mountain. When we went there in the morning any photo shots would have been directly into the sun.

I needed to ask questions. We saw stray dogs and loose sheep, but could not find any stores open in Truchas. Therefore, we went to the post office. A postal employee said that he had been to the top of North Truchas Peak. Yes, the rocks on the top are very sharp, but he was not sure that they were sharp enough to lance boils. However, obsidian found nearby, which Indians used to make razor **sharp stone** arrowheads, certainly should be able to do that.

The postal employee and another man there confirmed the report I had read that there were miles of old aqueducts chiseled into the rock of North Truchas. However, they both insisted that those locations were impossible for us to try to reach except with a 4-wheel drive vehicle.

At some time in the past those channels brought water down from the mountains to Truchas. Later when I talked to a park ranger near Albuquerque, although he had not been to that location, he denied that those aqueducts could possibly exist. It just was not in character what he knew about New Mexico. However, a park ranger elsewhere said that he, too, had been there and confirmed that he had seen the aqueducts (acequias).

Some credit the early Spanish settlers with building those aqueducts. Were they credited for that as they were for the supposed "Spanish diggings" in Wyoming because people did not know who else could have built them?

Even before 2000 BC Chinese were diverting water. Could Chinese have built them? Ironically, the story goes that at the same time the Spanish built the aqueducts, Truchas was also walled to protect itself from the marauding Apache and Comanche Indians. It would have been difficult to fight off Indians and chisel rock for so many miles at the same time.

The New Mexico Office of the State Historian wrote that flood-water farming and other irrigation practices were conducted by some of the indigenous people who preceded the Spanish. That office credits the acequias to the Spanish.[82]

After North Truchas we drove south. It seemed that most of the buildings in New Mexico were adobe (a modern form of wattle and daub), which was quite different from most structures in Colorado. We passed lots of Indian reservations and casinos. Decorations on highway walls and overpasses are unique.

We drove about an hour west of Albuquerque to Acoma, a Native American pueblo. Reportedly built around AD 1100, Acoma is the "oldest continuously inhabited village in the United States"[83] and is a National Historic Landmark.

Acoma is on top of this mesa

8 – North Truchas Peak, New Mexico

After we turned off the main highway and traveled toward the pueblo, unfenced (presumably wild) ponies grazed along the road. Bear, elk, pronghorn, and mountain lions also roam the almost half a million acre reservation. Acoma sits atop a 367 foot tall sandstone mesa. The people living there still have no electricity or running water. Gardens are in the valley below.

The tour is well worth the time and expense to see their village and hear about their history. The residents were living on this mesa in 1539 when Francisco Vasques de Coronado's expedition came through. Later the Spanish viewed the mesa in the light of the sunset. It glowed like gold and the Spanish were sure that this must be one of the seven fabled cities of gold.

After a series of conflicts with the Spanish, in 1599 the mesa was attacked and the Spanish prevailed. At that time at the order of the Spanish, all the males over 25 years old had their right foot cut off. Everyone 12 years and over was sentenced to 20 years of slavery. The Spanish speaking judge ordered that children under 12 have a Catholic upbringing under a Franciscan priest. Sixty girls from Acoma were forcibly taken from their families and sent to Mexico City, never to be seen again.

Later a Catholic church was built on Acoma mesa. Seventy four men and women died in the construction of the church, which still stands there. Reportedly most of those are buried within the walls of that building.

Acoma at sunrise - © Baker Aerial Archaeology

Years later the people from Acoma were part of the Pueblo Revolt of 1680, in which many different Native American tribes united to successfully gain independence from the Spanish tyrants.

As I read *Indian Uprising on the Rio Grande: The Pueblo Revolt of 1680*, I was struck by how some of the Native American customs paralleled those in China. The Indians used smoke signals to communicate. They offered food to the dead. In *Secret Maps of the Ancient World* I mention many more correlations of Chinese customs to those of Native Americans.

Some of the houses in Acoma today are three stories high with ladders going up. The guide pointed out that some of the ceilings of first floors were low by today's standards. He stated that the early people were quite short – several inches less than 5 feet tall. They are a matriarchal society with the house going to the youngest daughter of the family.

Today only a few live there. Most have a home with modern conveniences in another location. A few people at a time stay in Acoma to sustain the history of continuous occupation.

8 – North Truchas Peak, New Mexico

Acoma

Did Ancient Chinese Explore America?

On their web site they refer to themselves as Acoma (pronounced with a hard c), but also as "Y'aak'a" and the museum as "Haak'u Museum." Those last spellings made me wonder whether the people of Acoma were related to the Hakka people, a hardworking Chinese ethnic group I met during my teen years in Hong Kong. Hakka were known throughout Chinese history for their far flung travels.

Unlike the musical tones of Mandarin, I recall that the Hakka ethnic language was pronounced with deep guttural sounds – as surely "Haak'u" would be. (As a youngster who grew up with the softer tones of Mandarin, those Hakka guttural sounds made me nervous that someone was getting ready to spit in my direction.)

Technically Hakka are not a matriarchal society, but Hakka women usually are the ones in charge of both the family home and business, leaving the men free for other pursuits like politics. The Hakka are also short in stature.

Hakka today live in modern cities. *Encyclopedia.com* indicates that Hakka of old built: "circular or rectangular, multistoried, fortress like dwellings, designed for defensive purposes….made of adobe or tampered earth."[84] Those houses had walls nearly a meter think and were three or four stories high. That is similar to the houses at Acoma. However, the technical comparison of Hakka to Haak'u will have to be a study for another scholar.

The native tour guide, a bright young college student, related that some from Acoma served in the US armed forces during various conflicts. A grave from WWII is in the church cemetery. Someone from the audience asked why they would voluntarily serve in the US military, considering their previous treatment by the white men. "We love this country and the freedoms that the United States gives us," replied the guide.

Later, when reading my manuscript for this book, my brother Hendon asked, "Could Acoma have been the Land of Women?" I had not considered that before. Today there are other female led native groups in the vicinity of Acoma, but Hendon pointed out that in most cultures a matriarchal society is unusual.

Our father's maps show the Land of Women inland from the West Coast of what we now refer to as America. Father wrote about the Land of Women mentioned in the *Shan Hai Jing*[85] and he also stated that early Spanish explorers looked for it.

Chao Chien, under the pen name Anatole Andro, wrote that a 16th century Spanish book, *Las Sergas de Esplandian,* identified California as an island inhabited by women.[86] In *Secret Maps of the Ancient World* I quoted another reputable early Chinese reference to Land of Women.[87]

Mertz cited a Chinese court record from about AD 502 that referenced the Land of Women.[88] According to the distances given in that writing, Mertz placed it about 350 miles inland from the coast. She conjectured that it might have been on a Mogollon mesa in east or central Arizona.[89] It is interesting that she placed it on a mesa.

Acoma mesa today is 600 miles inland from the Pacific Ocean and only about 120 miles from Arizona. According to the history of the Acoma they moved to their current location from elsewhere. Of course, I cannot prove that Acoma is the Land of Women, but that is a possibility.

About 80 miles due north of Acoma is Chaco Canyon. There sits unexplained evidence of an advanced people and prehistoric astronomers from 700 or more years ago. *Ancient Treasures of the Southwest* states:

> In the Chaco Canyon area of New Mexico ingenious ancient astronomers constructed a sophisticated calendrical device on top of a high butte. In this observatory large slabs of rock were arranged so that shafts of sunlight fell between them onto a group of spiral markings carved into a cliff wall. As the position of the sun changed with the season, the shafts of light traversed the face of the markings, indicating important dates to those who knew how to read them.
>
> Skeptical archeologists at first found it hard to believe....but after careful study they could find no reason to doubt that this was a true astronomical device invented by some Chacoan genius – or geniuses....Because of recent deterioration, the Park Service has closed Fajada Butte to all visitation.[90]

The people in Chaco Canyon (the Anasazi) had great houses made of stone imported from other areas and over 300 miles of excellent road system. Some of the roads were over 30 feet wide. The main road ran due north/south and cut through low hills. This appears to have been a major trading center including trade with Central America. They had irrigation and gardens of their own.

The Anasazi arrived there about the same time as the people at Acoma. Although by then advanced astronomical devices were in use for thousands of years in Asia, the writer of *Ancient Treasurers of the Southwest* seemed unwilling to believe anything except that the device in Chaco Valley had been re-invented right there by a Chacoan genius.

Dave and I spent the next three nights in Los Lunas, outside of Albuquerque because of its central location and economical lodging. It was nice having a couple of days respite from dragging suitcases in and out of motels.

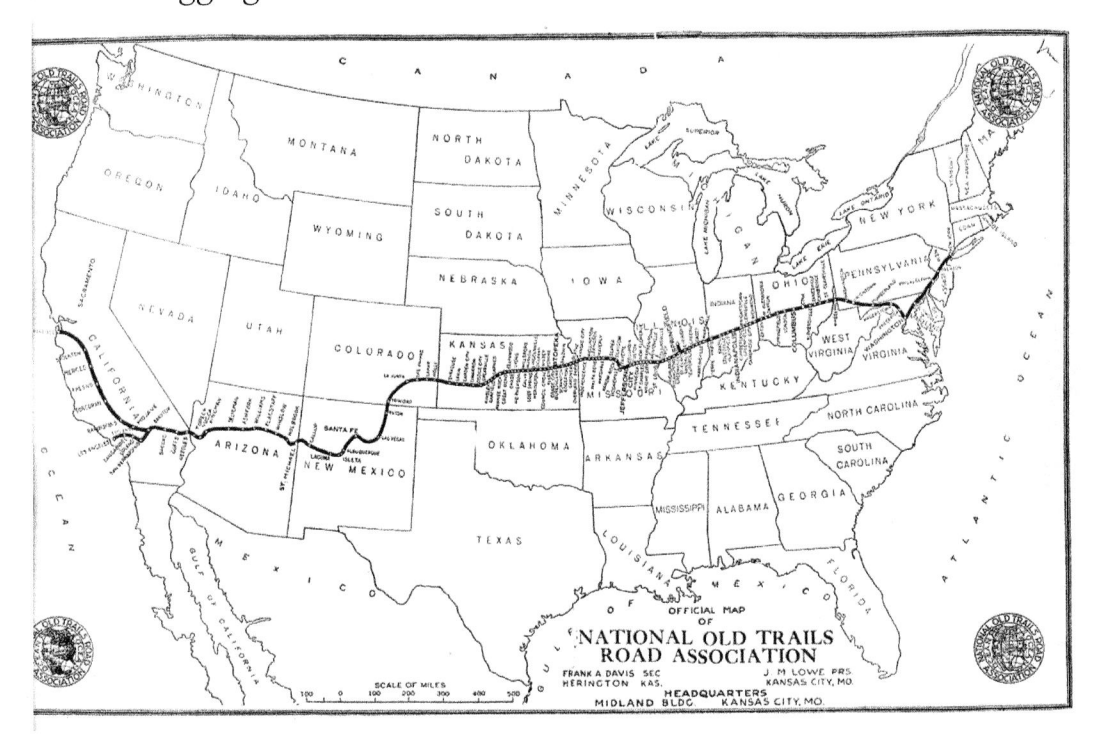

The famous US Route 66 which runs through Los Lunas was originally proposed to run from coast to coast – which would have covered around 3300 miles. When completed in the early 20th century it ran 2451 miles from Chicago in America's Midwest to the West Coast, still a huge feat. In the early 1950s, when my family crossed the US from Chicago to California as we set out for Taiwan, we surely went through Los Lunas on Route 66. At that time there were few other good cross country routes. Route 66 was also known as National Old Trails Road. One section of those ancient trails used by Route 66 took travelers past Acoma to the Pacific.

The width of the US is 3000 to 3400 miles, depending on the latitude at which the measurement is taken. In the third century BC, Tong Fang Tso of China wrote that Fu Sang was 10,000 li (approximately 3300 miles) wide then one comes to another immense ocean.[91] Perhaps the Chinese people who long ago measured the width of Fu Sang formed the original trails beneath Route 66. Today Interstate 40 (I-40) covers most of the roads that were previously known as Route 66.

After the manuscript to this book was completed, I asked Dr. John Ruskamp to read it. He told me at that time that many of the petroglyphs of ancient Chinese writing that he has found are across several states and near the western portion of I-40. His findings have been verified by other experts as ancient Chinese.

Historic Express St. James Hotel in Cimarron, New Mexico, another Santa Fe Trail site and a National Historic Landmark, is just a few miles further north, a short distance from the Colorado state line. "Cimarron" is the Spanish word for "wild" or "unruly" and the town lived up to its name.

Established in 1872, Express St. James Hotel has a history of several gunfights in which a total of 26 people were killed over a period of time. The hotel, which some claim is haunted, and the restaurant are still in operation. Bullet holes can still be seen in the ceiling of the bar there. Buffalo Bill Cody stayed there as well as outlaws Black Jack Ketchum and Jesse James and lawmen the Earp brothers.[93]

There were two branches to the Santa Fe Trail. Most interesting to me of everything on the eastern side of North Truchas Peak was that the mountain route of the Santa Fe Trail went through there and that it followed old Indian trails.

In 1801 a Blackfoot chief drew a map of "the world" for Hudson Bay Company. *Landscapes of Movement: Trails, Paths, and Roads in Anthropological Perspective* explains:

> This map which encompasses a 1,200 square mile area virtually unknown to White explorers, depicts a portion of the "Old North Trail" that ran parallel to the Rocky Mountain Front from the Upper Saskatchewan River in Alberta to, arguably, the city of Santa Fe in New Mexico (Ewers 1980). This map also sketches the Missouri River watershed, from the Continental Divide to the mouth of the Yellowstone River, noting the existence of the river villages just to the east of this landmark....[this] map became the key to the Western territories as it depicted the route Lewis and Clark would soon follow.[94]

I have not been able to find out how long the Old North Trail was in use or whether the Santa Fe Trail later traced that exact route. However, the 1801 map shows much of the same area as that covered in this particular *Shan Hai Jing* journey. (See the map on the facing page.)

If the *Shan Hai Jing* travelers did not follow the Rio Grande south from Blanca Peak to North Truchas on the western side of the mountain range, they could have gone down the eastern side to North Truchas and almost to our next stop, Manzano Peak, by following those old Indian trails.

The fact that at North Truchas and at several other stops the *Shan Hai Jing* mentioned a river or stream that flowed to the east, seems to imply that the Chinese explored the eastern side of these mountains. Perhaps the Chinese were the ones who originally made those trails.

9 – Manzano Peak, New Mexico

And it says that, three hundred li to the south, YOH (Lofty) Mountain is found. Upon this there are many **mulberry-trees**, and below it many **ailanthus-trees**. LOH River is found here, a **stream flowing easterly into a marsh**, and in it there are **many gems and much gold**. (Vining translation of *Shan Hai Jing*)

Mertz note:

> The "Lofty" mountain is Manzano Peak, high point in the range of the same name. The stream flowing into a marsh was not identifiable on my map. There may be one that is not large enough to be shown – or the possibility exists that one may have dried up in the intervening 4,000 years. Climatic conditions, according to scientists, apparently changed in this specific area within the past 700-800 years, since many Indian sites, of an early age, show an exodus from here about 1200 – 1300 A.D., presumably caused by draught (sic) or some climatic change.

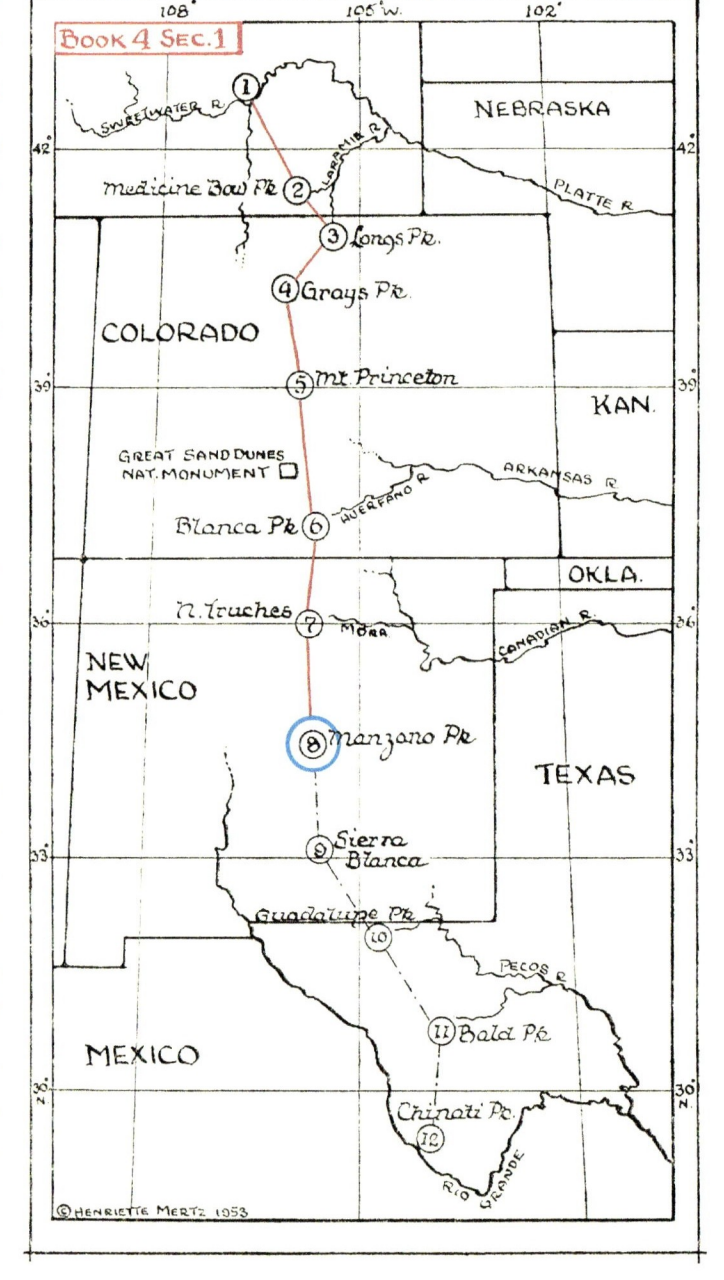

Did Ancient Chinese Explore America?

As we approached Manzano State Park a storm came up with a tremendous display of lightening and rain. That was followed by the most beautiful and vivid double rainbow that Dave and I had ever seen. We were able to view all of both rainbows. They filled the sky. Dave, who usually is sedate, was so awestruck that he stopped the car in the middle of the road and jumped out to take photos. (Fortunately we were on a country road with no other traffic.) Both he and I were rejoicing and praising God. The Manzano State Park was closed for the season, but the rainbow was a foreshadow of what I was to find there.

On the internet I found an exhaustive academic survey of plants in the Sandia and Manzano Mountians.[101] Among those listed is not only the wild apple tree (malus pumila) but also wild pear trees (pyrus communis), both native to China. In looking through the list of plants, I noticed that the biologist indicated that 108 of those

Did Ancient Chinese Explore America?

Anderson wrote:

> The pre-Columbian diet of central Mexico….a form of millet (Setaria viridis) similar to Chinese foxtail millet came first but was abandoned when maize came into favor.

> Mexico could have grown millet on lands too dry or cold for maize, as China did, but the competitive advantage of doing so was apparently too small to make it worthwhile….Maize provided the most calories per acre and was the staple.[105]

Mexico borders New Mexico. Maize was in New Mexico by around 2000 BC.

I was very surprised to find that the remaining nine of those 93 non-native Asian plants in the Manzano Mountains were varieties of Chinese grasses that could have been used for animal feed. Even though a scientist in China helped me search, we could not find any other use for those grasses.[106] Would that suggest that perhaps the early travelers brought horses or found horses in North America?

Dr. Arthur H. Harris (no relationship to me) of the University of Texas at El Paso wrote that horses are native to North America. He stated:

> Horse teeth and lower-leg bones...probably are the commonest fossils brought into the university and schools of the area for identification.[107]

Arthur Harris contends that horses died out in North America long before 2000 BC. In *Secret Maps of the Ancient World* I discussed multiple evidences of pre-Columbian equine in North America including horse bones from Wisconsin that carbon dated to AD 750-900.[108] Numerous other drawings of horses in the Americas are dated to pre-Columbian times.

There is both written and archeological proof that in China people were riding horses by 2000 BC.[109] The stone anchors found by Bob Meistrell and others mentioned in Chapter 2 would suggest sizeable boats which would have been needed if the early Chinese brought horses to America.

The fourteenth book of the *Shan Hai Jing* does not give specific distances between landmarks, so it was not charted by Mertz. However, it references horses in what is thought to be North America.[110] In fact, one of those horse descriptions is strikingly similar to Appaloosa. (Appaloosa horses are shown in Chinese art which pre-dates Columbus.) The early sixth century Chinese account of Hui Shen's trip to Fu Sang also mentions horses.[111]

On the way up, the tram operator pointed out Totem Rock. It is said to be a natural formation, but looks like a totem pole. Though it appears to be stacked rocks, we were told that it is all connected and is the equivalent of a seven storey building.

I could not help but recall that from extremely early dates that there were totem poles in China. It is said that Chinese invented the totem pole. Even the word "totem" is Chinese. A totem pole in China at Sichuan Province Sanxingdui archeological site is dated to 2050 BC.[115] There is still a totem pole today in Tiananmen Square.

In 1973 my father, Dr. Hendon Harris, Jr. stated in *The Asiatic Fathers of America:* "The record of Asia is written into the stones of America and into the bodies of its early people."

Totem Rock

Now DNA establishes the connection of Native Americans to Asians. Petroglyphs, which, of course, are written on stone, are all over America's Southwest.

At the edge of Albuquerque to the northwest of Manzano Peak we visited Boca Negra Canyon, which is part of Petroglyph National Monument. There carved on black volcanic rock are over 20,000 petroglyphs. According to a brochure from the National Park Service:

> Archeologists, currently using relative dating methods along the escarpment are arriving at the conclusion that the petroglyphs were created between circa 1000 BC and the 1700s. Many contemporary American

Did Ancient Chinese Explore America?

Often a Chinese written word is made up from several pictograms called radicals. For instance, the pictogram for guo (fruit tree) is the drawing for mu (tree) with fruit with a seed in it added at the top. Ruskamp noted that the character for hua (flower) shown below also has the character tu (ground) attached at the bottom of the flower.[121] Perhaps this designated a live flower.

Is it coincidence that in this area with unexplained apple trees, early cultigens, and Chinese medicinal plants, that so many of these seven ancient pictograms shown by Ruskamp refer to crop cultivation? In Ruskamp's main text he has a whole chapter dedicated to "North American Botanical Pictograms." Over time as the thousands of petroglyphs near Albuquerque are studied, surely even more will be recognized as Chinese pictograms.

If you go to Petroglyph National Monument in Albuquerque, stop at the Park Service office at 6001 Unser Boulevard for brochures and instructions. One can walk right in among the petroglyphs to view them.

Photos from *Asiatic Echoes The Identification of Chinese Pictograms in North American Rock Writing Addendum 2012*, Courtesy of John A. Ruskamp, Jr.

Just five months before we visited Albuquerque when I had speeches in Europe, Dave and I visited Paris and the Louvre. It is breathtaking to tour the Louvre and see priceless works of art such as the Mona Lisa and Venus de Milo. Yet the petroglyphs in New Mexico date back much earlier in time and are also irreplaceable art.

9 – Manzano Peak, New Mexico

As we ascended one hill in Boca Negra Canyon we were met by a young family descending. The son of that family, about age 7, had a check list and was marking off petroglyphs that he was supposed to see for a school project. However, he expressed disappointment. When we asked why, he replied that "a live snake" was on his checklist and he had not seen one. We noted signs to beware of rattlesnakes and were glad that none crossed our path. However, unfortunately the value of those petroglyphs was lost to the young boy in his quest for a snake.

The Native Americans regard these petroglyphs as sacred. *Petroglyph National Monument* quotes Laurie Weakhee, a Native American:

> The volcanic escarpment is the centerpiece of a larger belief structure incorporating the highest peaks of surrounding mountain ranges, all of which can be seen from the escarpments. Because of the centrality of this site in the universe of other sacred sites, it has long been the object of what other religions would view as pilgrimages. This area is connected by ancient pathways to a larger network of pilgrimage routes throughout the Southwest.[122]

Mountains mentioned by Weakhee in that text as visible from Boca Negra include Sandia and Manzano Peaks.

Currently there are more than 175,000 listed archeological sites in New Mexico from numerous time periods. Most of them are from the last 1000 years. However, *Prehistoric New Mexico* noted an archaic site from around 2000 BC at Boca Negra Cave[123] and another from around that same time at a cave on Manzano.[124]

Of course, 2000 BC is the same time period that Mertz contends for the *Shan Hai Jing*. Since stone cannot be carbon dated, the dating of the objects in the Boca Negra Cave might give a more accurate dating for the earliest petroglyphs there at Petroglyph National Monument than the estimated date by the National Park Service shown earlier in this chapter.

Paleoindian sites in the Rio Grande Valley of New Mexico, said to predate the archaic, are normally in a specific pattern. According to W. James Judge in *Paleoindian Occupation: of the Central Rio Grande Valley in New Mexico*:

> Paleoindian sites were generally located on ridges near playas (frequently to the northeast of a playa)....frequently there was a major drainage nearby.[125]

Merriam Webster Online defines playa as: "A flat-floored bottom of an undrained desert basin that becomes at times like a shallow lake." This implied that the opening of those paleoindian dwellings would have faced south and the water would have also been to the south.

I find this orientation very interesting because this positioning is according to the principles of Feng Shui. This Chinese geomantic belief system states that for optimal prosperity structures should be oriented to the south with mountains to the north and the dwelling facing a river or water source.

Feng Shui is from the ancient Chinese religion of Taoism. Taoism had no founding date and no founder,[126] but according to "History of Taoism" it: "stretches throughout Chinese history. Originating in prehistoric China, it has exerted a powerful influence over Chinese culture throughout the ages."[127]

The University of Washington states:

> One of the most striking aspects of Chinese domestic architecture is the practice of making houses face south.... many neolithic-period houses were rectangular with a south-facing door.[128]

John B. Carlson in "A Geomantic Model for the Interpretation of Mesoamerican Sites" mentioned similar south facing orientation in other regions of the Americas.

High Rolls Cave, which is just south of our next *Shan Hai Jing* stop, was dated to 3500 years ago, and contained cultigens. The opening of High Rolls cave is toward the south and a body of water.[129] I have not yet been able to find whether other archaic home sites of New Mexico also had the same positioning.

However, the Henderson Site burials near Roswell, New Mexico dated AD 1200 -1400 had the heads of almost all the deceased facing south and overlooking a river, which would also be according to the rules of Feng Shui. Furthermore, the Henderson Site burials included decorated animal scapula, cultivated crops, red ocher, and numerous Olivella shells. Some of the human teeth were shovel shaped and a few of the heads had artificial cranial deformation.[130] All those items or characteristics, especially when viewed together, could point to China.

Albuquerque is known for its yearly hot air balloon festival that spans two weekends in the fall. Brightly colored balloons fill the sky. Unfortunately, Dave and I missed those dates, but saw several hot air balloons early one morning. On Sandia Peak is a memorial to two balloonists from Chicago who crossed both the Atlantic and the Pacific Oceans using balloons.

According the Joseph Needham and Robert Temple, by the fourth century BC Chinese had manned flight with kites and by the second century BC had miniature hot air balloons.[131]

At another stop in Texas, later on this same *Shan Hai Jing* journey, we discuss how aerial photography is needed to capture the complete designs of some of the ancient rock art there. Surely no artist would design a masterpiece that he could not later step back to admire. Furthermore, one of the repeated designs in the rock art in Texas is shown and described as "diamond shape with tail."[132] If we drew it today, we would call that a kite.

Of course, the earliest Chinese explorers to New Mexico would not have utilized kites or balloons, but I and many others believe that there were many crossings of the Pacific over a long period of time. Perhaps at later dates Chinese used their technology of flight in this very area. If so, the sandy, flat valleys of New Mexico and West Texas would have afforded soft landings.

10 – Sierra Blanca, New Mexico

And it says that, three hundred li to the south, **Wolf Mountain** is to be found. Upon this there is **no grass** and there are **no trees**, and below it there is much water (or there are **many streams**), in which there are many **KAN-TSZ fish**. [These are not fully described.] They have wild animals, which look like the (quadrumana, called) **KW'A-FU**, but they have hair like that of swine and their voice is like an expiration of the breath. When these are seen, then heaven sends down great rains. (Vining translation of *Shan Hai Jing*)

Mertz note:

> 95 miles south of Manzano is Sierra Blanca, with many noisy streams chasing down its slopes – two main tributaries flow into the Rio Hondo. The wild animals that look like swine and are the size of monkey, I am not able to identify – they may be small peccary.

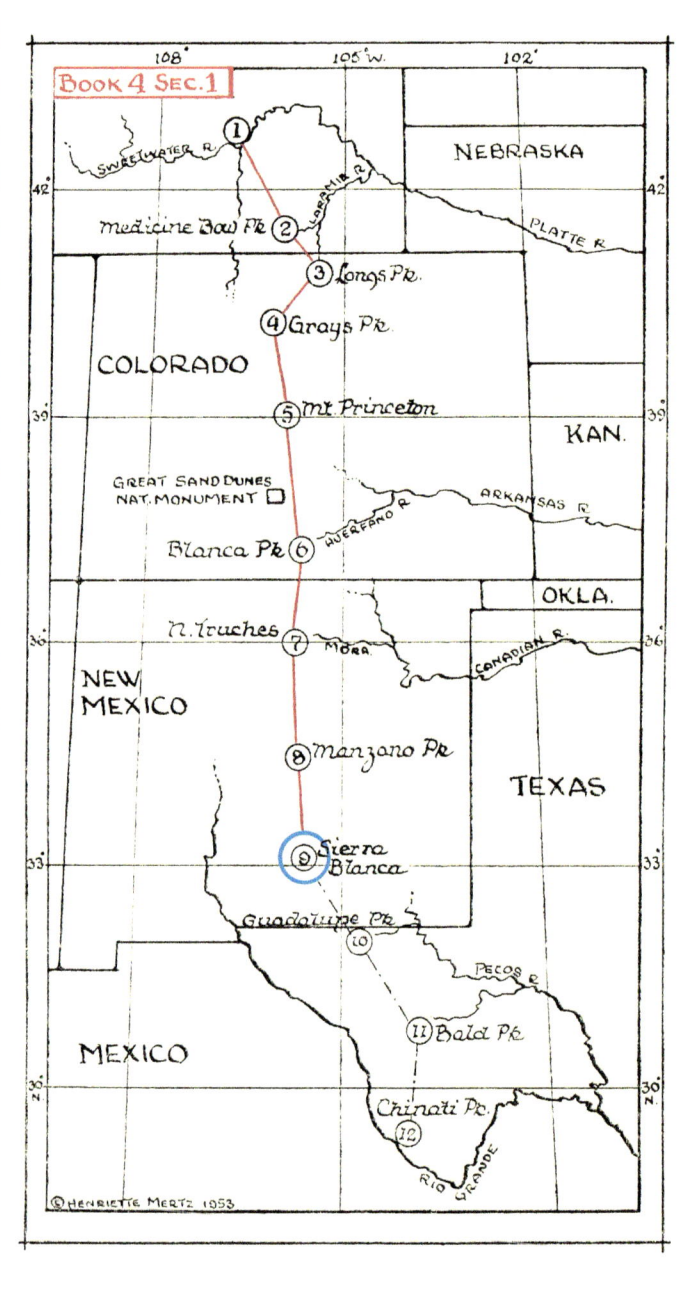

Author's Comments:

As previously stated, "Blanca" means "white" in Spanish. Sierra Blanca is also known as

- 92 -

White Mountain. According to the Mescalero Apache web site:

> The range is about 40 miles from north to south and 20 miles wide, and is dominated by Sierra Blanca Peak….much of the southern half of the range, including the summit of Sierra Blanca Peak, is part of the Mescalero Apache Indian Reservation, and requires a permit for access.[133]

"Sierra Blanca is a significant sacred site in Mescalero Apache culture."[134] Although the Mescalero Apache web site says that access is only by permit, since 1963 that tribe has operated a resort now called Ski Apache on Sierra Blanca. The tram ride up is said to be spectacular. From the resort are several miles of hiking trails.[135]

The Chinese named this "**Wolf Mountain.**" That would seem to imply that they saw wolves there.

Wolves – courtesy of National Park Service

Wolf tracks courtesy of National Park Service

Gray wolves (canis lupus) in North America originally had a range from the arctic down to Mexico,[136] but today are usually found only in far northern areas.

An analysis of the petroglyphs of the Sierra Blanca region by Dr. Robert H. Weber of the New Mexico Bureau of Mines and Mineral Resources mentions that among the petroglyphs: "Tracks of bear and wolf are… clearly delineated."[137] To correctly draw wolf tracks, the artist had to have seen real wolf tracks, and probably even wolves. The oldest petroglyphs of that area are thought to date back to around AD 900.

Did Ancient Chinese Explore America?

Zooarchaeology of Six Prehistoric Sites in the Sierra Blanca Region, New Mexico studied areas thought to be from AD 1100 – 1450. They found coyote and dog bones, but specifically stated that they found nothing large enough to classify as wolf. Perhaps the wolves had died out by then. If so, one might conclude that whoever made the wolf tracks on the petroglyphs did so before AD 1100 and that if the Chinese really did make this *Shan Hai Jing* journey they were there before the wolves died out, also.

Microbiologist Dr. Simon Southerton stated in *Losing a Lost Tribe*:

> Mitochondrial studies suggest the New World dogs were faithful companions during the early settlement of the Americas. DNA sequences obtained from pre-Columbian dog remains in Latin America and Alaska have been compared to the DNA of dogs and wolves from around the world…and it is now clear that New World dogs occupy the same branch of the canine family trees as modern Eurasian dogs. The American gray

Photo courtesy of NPS

> wolf is a distant cousin. It would appear that when humans crossed…into the Americas, they were accompanied by their canine companions.[138]

Sierra Blanca Peak sits at 11,973 feet and is also part of the Sangre de Cristo range of the Rocky Mountains. As the *Shan Hai Jing* described, the top of Sierra Blanca Peak **has no grass and no trees.** Today locals call it "Old Baldy." However, there are several different life zones found on the mountain. Various plants and trees can be found growing up to certain elevations.[139] As with other mountains on this range, the western slope is much more barren than the eastern.

10 – Sierra Blanca, New Mexico

When driving there from Los Lunas where we were staying, this location seemed very remote. On one side of the highway for many miles as we drove east then south was a huge missile range. It is considerable distance between houses. After all, who would choose to live next to a missile range?

It had rained two days earlier. Many flowers of various colors including red, orange, white, and yellow bloomed next to the highway in this otherwise desolate region. We drove through an area where the rocks were all black. Later we learned that this was called "Valley of the Fires." Reportedly it was caused by a volcanic eruption only a thousand years ago.[140]

After almost three hours of driving, we finally arrived at the small town of Carrizo where we stopped at a convenience store. The school mascot there is a grizzly bear.

Mountain Lion courtesy of NPS

Someone had painted its depiction on the wall of the store. I asked if there are still grizzlies there. The store clerk replied that because of the drought, bears from the mountains had been showing up in town lately in the middle of the day. Those bears making appearances in Carrizo may be distant relatives of the famous Smokey the Bear, a cub saved from a forest fire in nearby Capitan Gap in 1950.[141]

There are bears there, but according to a park ranger, no more grizzlies. Other large animals in that part of New Mexico include mountain lions weighing up to 190 pounds. The internet displayed the photo of a large one in this area recently shot by hunters. Even up in the Sandia Mountains, which are much closer to heavily populated areas, in 2008 a young child was picked up by a mountain lion, but was released relatively unharmed.

The **KAN TSZ'** named here appears to be the same fish (trout) mentioned at Mt. Princeton and Blanca Peak.

Fly Fishing in Southern New Mexico states:

> Rio Ruidoso is a small freestone river originating on the southern slope of 12,000 foot Sierra Blanca, 10 miles west of Ruidoso, New Mexico. It starts as three forks joining together on the Mescalero Apache Indian Reservation then flows through the city of Ruidoso east to its confluence to the Rio Bonito where the Rio Hondo is formed.[142]

That text indicates that brown trout are found there in a 35 mile long section of Carrizo Creek and Rio Ruidoso.

We previously mentioned that the US Geological Survey (USGS), a scientific agency of the US government, indicates that brown trout are not native to the Americas and that they sometimes replace the native fish. That study also stated that natural reproduction of brown trout is low or nonexistent in most states.[143]

However, the local web site for the City of Ruidoso indicates that while other trout are restocked in the local streams, brown trout there are not restocked because Carrizo Creek is Ruidoso's natural hatchery and nursery for them.

They have become so acclimated there that this web site referred to brown trout as "native."[144] Even if the brown trout there now have replaced the native fish, this seems an ideal spot for that species.

The *Shan Hai Jing* describes **many streams** at Sierra Blanca. As stated above, Rio Ruidoso has three main forks flowing east from Sierra Blanca. Rio Ruidoso translates from Spanish as "noisy river," presumably the noise was from water rushing down the slopes. If one views Sierra Blanca Peak, New Mexico on Google Maps, he will

Three Rivers Petroglyphs in foreground & Sierra Blanca in background

10 – Sierra Blanca, New Mexico

see several more streams and rivers that flow down the west side of that mountain. Three Rivers Petroglyph Site is near where three westward flowing rivers from that mountain range converge.

Dave and I walked through the delightful petroglyphs of the Three Rivers Petroglyph Site and photographed Sierra Blanca from there. This petroglyph site is under the

protection of the Bureau of Land Management. It boasts more than 21,000 glyphs scattered over 50 acres of desert. They are thought to date back to AD 900-1400 and are attributed to Jornada Mogollon. However, not far away are two different archaic sites, Alamagordo and Parabolic Dune Hearth Mounds which have each been dated to 2000 BC. Alamagordo had a large amount of perishable material that was tested.[145]

Weber wrote concerning the Three Rivers Petroglyphs:

> The figures are highly varied and may be of more than one age. Among the forms noted are realistic, stylized human figures, heads, handprints, footprints, and possible mythical beings, corn plants…geometric pat-

terns....Among the animal figures are birds in flight and at rest (a highly realistic quail, roadrunners, turkeys, possible macaws, and others). Lizards, frogs, turtles, snakes, beetles, butterflies, worms, fish, deer (a spotted fawn is especially noteworthy), rabbits, chipmunk, skunk, mountain lions, and mountain sheep. Tracks of birds are common: some are aligned in trails that trip lightly across the tops of boulders....Human figures are largely stylized stick and solid forms of considerable variety. Goggle-eyed faces are repeated at several places....Masks and headdresses are indicated on several figures ....Cultural affiliations of the Three Rivers petroglyphs have not been established.[146]

Among the petroglyphs at Three Rivers is a very Asian looking face. At this site we saw more petroglyphs with less walking than at Boca Negra Canyon.

I disagree with Mertz in her conjecture of what **KW'A-FU** was. The *Shan Hai Jing* described it as an animal that looked like a quadrumana (a primate, a monkey). Mertz guessed that the animal described by the Chinese was a peccary – an animal in the pig family.

Further south on this same *Shan Hai Jing* journey, at Baldy Peak, Texas the Chinese mention another animal which Mertz also thought was peccary. I believe Mertz had the correct interpretation for that animal in Texas. However, the Chinese name in the *Shan Hai Jing* for the animal at Sierra Blanca and the one at Baldy Peak are different. Surely if the Chinese saw another similar animal on that single trip they would have named it identically as they did with the KAN-TSZ fish.

As Mertz knew, peccary are occasionally found in the vicinity of Sierra Blanca. Just a few days after Dave and I were in that area, the news reported that a wild peccary with razor sharp tusks, which could have destroyed a pet dog in seconds, was discovered walking down the street in Ruidoso and was shot by a police officer.

I could not find evidence of peccary there in the distant past. However, my main argument against peccary is that they look nothing like monkeys. Note that the *Shan Hai Jing* says that the animals looked like monkeys but had hair like swine.

As a child in Taiwan I played with my family's pet monkey and dressed it up in doll clothes. One of the peculiarities of monkeys is that their feet are similar to hands. My pet liked to suck his thumb or his big toe. Monkeys have a distinct way of walking that is similar to a bear or a human in that their entire foot touches the ground. This foot posture, called plantigrade, is not real common in animals.

Yellow Bellied Marmot photo courtesy NPS

There is an animal living in the area of Sierra Blanca and native to America which does have plantigrade foot posture.[147] It stands almost the same way that monkeys do. Yellow bellied marmot (marmota flaviventris), which is in the rodent or squirrel family, could be compared to a fat monkey. This animal is native to the Americas. It whistles or chirps or makes a chucking sound when startled. It has lots of hair like a monkey, but the hair is coarse – like that of a pig, as the *Shan Hai Jing* contended.

Marmots are found in the Sangre de Cristo Mountains in New Mexico. Palaeoecological results from that area confirm the presence of marmots there at very early dates.[148]

11 – Guadalupe Mountains, Texas

And it says that, three hundred li to the south, **Lone Mountain** is found. Upon this there are **many gems and much gold**, and below it **many beautiful stones. MOH-T'U (Muddy) River** is found here, a **stream flowing southeasterly** into a mighty flood, in which there are many **T'IAO-YUNG**. These look like **yellow serpents with fish's fins**. They go out and in. They are bright (or smooth). When these are seen, then that region is subject to great drought. (Vining translation of *Shan Hai Jing*)

Mertz Note:

> South from Sierra Blanca is Guadalupe, or "Lone" peak, highest point in Texas. Flowing southeast from the peak is Delaware Creek, emptying into the Pecos, which on occasion, floods. Again, there are many semi-precious stones, as well as gold, in the mountains. Guadalupe, identified as "Lone"

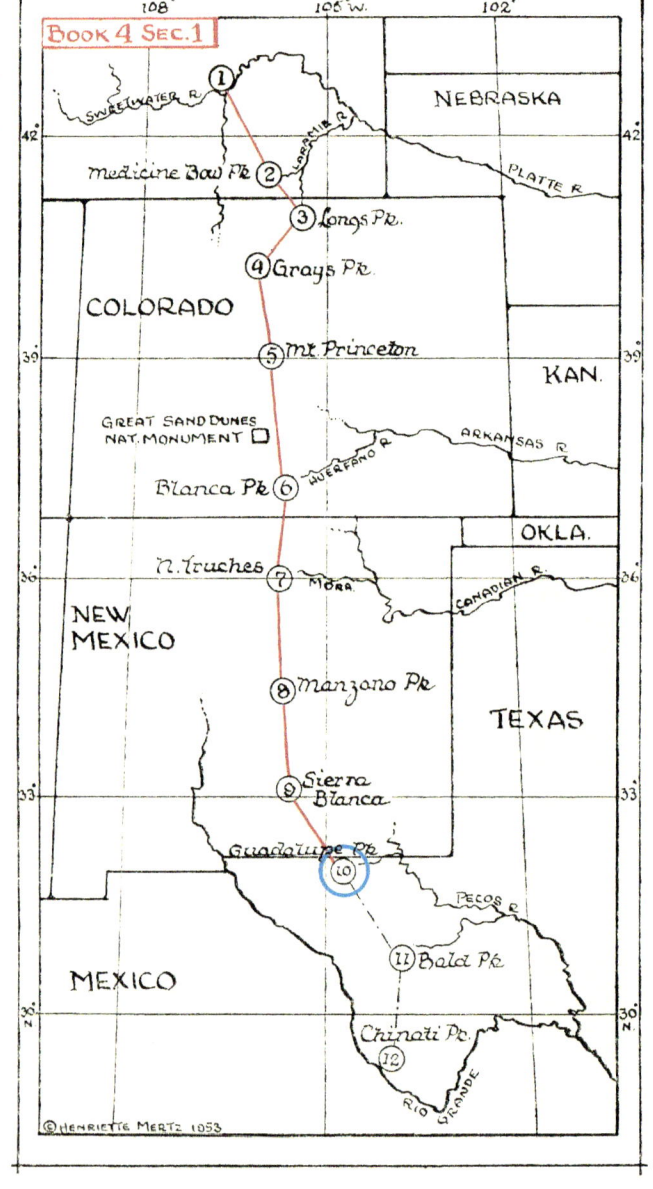

peak is the only one of considerable height in the area. Travelers, who had just come over the rugged terrain where towering peaks surrounded them at every turn, would spot this "lone" peak quickly.

11 – Guadalupe Mountains, Texas

Author's Comments:

My husband and I completed the first nine stops of this particular *Shan Hai Jing* journey down through New Mexico in 2012. The Texas part of this journey was done by my brother (Hendon Harris, III) and me in two trips in 2009. It was what we found there that led me to eventually complete the entire trek. Hendon would have loved to have experienced the whole trip, but could not take that much time off from work.

Both times Hendon and I went to Texas during the colder months. Snow was on the tops of many of the mountains of the rest of this journey so we could not access those other locations. I wanted to go to Texas when hopefully rattlesnakes there would be less active. Fortunately we did not encounter any snakes either time.

Hendon at Guadalupe Mountains National Park

Guadalupe Peak (8749 feet or 2,657 meters elevation), in Culberson County, is in the Trans-Pecos region of Texas, sometimes referred to as "West Texas." This peak, which is the tallest in the state, was once under water. Guadalupe Mountains National Park was established in 1972.

According the National Park Service there are over 300 caves in the Guadalupe Mountains. These caves are unique in beauty and geology. They have large limestone deposits which contain well-preserved marine fossils exposed during an uplift of the land.

> The Guadalupe Mountains are part of one of the finest examples of an ancient marine fossil reef on Earth. Geologists visit from around the world to marvel at this extraordinary natural phenomenon…[149]

Vining translated this "Lone Mountain." If Mertz named the correct mountain, one might wonder why it was named "Lone." Guadalupe Peak is close to the other Guadalupe Mountains and certainly is not alone.

El Capitan, Texas

I believe that the Chinese were describing El Capitan, which at 8085 feet or 2458 meters is not as high as Guadalupe Peak, but is the southern terminus of this range. As one approaches this area, El Capitan is an imposing sight as it rises straight up from the desert floor. On the western side of Guadalupe Peak and El Capitan are tons of gravel which in some areas is up to 600 feet deep.[150] Both Hendon and I wondered if that gravel was mine tailings but did not see other evidence of mines there.

Recently I asked a Chinese expert in ancient Chinese to re-translate this description. Without his knowledge of the geography of the area I was investigating, he wrote back. "Lone mountain is not a good translation….It should read 'the mountain that appears from the flat land.'" As I read that e-mail, my spine tingled because that exactly describes the mountains there.

The 2010 census record for Culberson County listed only 2398 people. The county has 3813 square miles. There is an average of 3.3 persons per household so if one spreads out all the households it would average over five square miles for each dwelling.

While some other areas of Texas have oil, this region does not. Outside of working on a ranch, in the tourist industry, or at the talc mine, not many local opportunities for employment exist. There are a lot of snakes and a trade in snake skins in Texas. Some men regularly capture live rattlesnakes for income.

According to the Texas Department of State Health Service about 7000 people in the USA suffer venomous snake bites annually, but only 1 or 2 people die each year in Texas from such bites.[151] Any bite by a venomous snake calls for immediate medical attention and possibly a painful hospitalization.

The Culberson County seat, Van Horn, has one grocery store and one dollar store, so some drive 120 miles to El Paso for their groceries.

In large cities around the world one can be lost in a crowd. Frequently neighbors in a metropolis do not even recognize each other. However, there is a deep sense of community in Culberson County and everybody knows the business (or thinks they do) of everyone else. Whoever you are, if you are around for long, your presence will be discussed by the locals.

Before I even visited this region the first time and was just booking a reservation at a bed and breakfast, the owner warned me that people for miles around would know whatever I did. They don't want anyone trespassing on their property without permission. West Texans are suspicious of strangers, love their guns, usually carry one with them, and aren't afraid to shoot. With that introduction from the proprietor of the B&B, which I assume she gave to everyone, I was amazed that she had other guests when we arrived.

However, this area has beautiful sunsets, and as the song goes, "The stars at night are big and bright…" The people that you get to know are on the whole friendly.

The **Delaware River flows east** from the Guadalupes into the Pecos River which in turn flows south, as the *Shan Hai Jing* stated.

The Trans-Pecos region is diverse. Higher elevations receive more precipitation and are wooded, but lower levels are scrub and arid desert grassland. The soils vary from deep sand to stony clay. Mountain ranges are either igneous or limestone.[152]

The *Shan Hai Jing* mentioned "**many gems**" at this location. Among the minerals of Culberson County are turquoise, copper, feldspar, barite, brines, gypsum, lead, zinc, mica, molybdenum, sulfur, and talc.[153]

Very little **gold** has been found in Texas. Traces were found in the Van Horn Mountains and other counties. However, rumors of gold in West Texas have circulated for a long time.

In "Secrets of the Guadalupes" from *Coronado's Children*, J. Frank Dobie (a university professor and prolific writer who had a personal war against those who "stretched" the truth) related some interesting accounts. Dobie wrote:

> The tradition of gold in the Guadalupes runs back a long, long way. While governor of New Mexico, General Lew Wallace…claimed in a written article…how a converted Indian of Tabira conducted Captain de Gavilan and thirty other Spaniards to a wonderfully rich gold deposit on the eastern spurs of the Guadalupe Mountains. The Spaniards named the place… Sierra de Cenizas…and left loaded down with nuggets and ore in the form of both "wires" and "masses." Then came the great uprising of 1680, in which the Pueblos killed every Spaniard who did not flee from New Mexico. About the same time Tabira, the home of the guide to Sierra de Cenizas, was wiped out. Sierra de Cenizas has for centuries been a lost spot in geography as well as a lost mine.[154]

Dobie contended that after that the Apaches also knew a location of gold in the Guadalupes. "Geronimo [famous Apache Chief] used to say that the richest gold mines in the western world lay hidden in the Guadalupes."

Among the accounts of gold in the Guadalupes, Dobie related the story of William Colum Sublett (better known as Ben Sublett).

Ben had prospected before, but he started again in the Guadalupes. This obsession kept him poor. Dobie wrote: "He could as the saying goes, live on what a hungry coyote would leave."

Eventually Ben moved his family to Odessa, Texas. His wife had died and he was gone for long periods of time looking for rumored gold in the Guadalupe Mountains. His destitute daughter took in washing to support the family. One day after being gone a long time Ben returned to Odessa.

Dobie stated:

> When Old Ben threw a pouch full of nuggets on the bar, the crowd went wild.
>
> "Boys," he said, "I have been poor, but I ain't poor no longer. I can buy out this town and have plenty left."
>
> "Drink."
>
> They drank. They cheered. They drank again. Then between drinks Old Ben went out to his buckboard and brought in a small canvas sack filled with gold "so pure a jeweler could have hammered it out." [155]

After that periodically Ben would slip out to the mountains alone and usually bring back about a thousand dollars worth of gold at a time. Many people tried to get him to tell where he had his cache, but Ben died not having told anyone, not even his family. Many witnesses in Odessa had seen him poor and then later saw his nuggets of gold.

An interesting clip from a 1958 TV series, which historically authenticates this story of Ben Sublett, can be seen on YouTube.[156]

Some predict that the next big gold find in North America will be in an area of Precambrian rock. Precambrian rock abounds in the Trans-Pecos region. I am unaware of any visible cauldrons in the area, but throughout the region there is a lot of evidence of volcanic activity in the distant past.

The Guadalupe Mountains are a botanist's paradise. *Studies in Vascular Plants, Mammal Survey, and Data Analysis, Guadalupe Mountains National Park, Texas* by Texas Tech University lists many unusual plants found in the park. Of the dozens of plants listed in this text that I also checked on *USDA Plants*, all are native. Several are found exclusively in this one county or only in that area.

Horned Lizard (Phrynosoma douglassi) courtesy of NPS

The Chinese wrote about **T'IAO-YUNG** which looked like **yellow serpents with fish's fins.** Perhaps this was a sighting of a small horned lizard (Phrynosoma douglassi), sometimes erroneously called horned toads, which are native to the area and found in the park. Some are yellowish on their sides and/or back and have small spikes sticking out from their heads, sides,

Did Ancient Chinese Explore America?

and spiny back – almost like the spiny dorsal fin of some fish. If T'IAO –YUNG is not the horned lizard, it could even be a now extinct reptile.

In *Secret Maps of the Ancient World* I mentioned examples of art in the Americas that depicted snakes with plumes or wings.[157] In fact, depictions of horned, plumed serpents are found in the Trans-Pecos region including one at Jaguar Cave in Alamo Canyon southeast of El Paso. As the crow flies that is only about 60 miles away from Guadalupe Peak.[158]

Horned Lizard (Phrynosoma douglassi) courtesy of NPS

Steep natural limestone walls have turned the tops of the Guadalupe Mountains into islands in the sky. High above the Chihuahuan Desert below, those walls set apart unique flora and fauna. *Studies in Vascular Plants, Mammal Survey, and Data Analysis, Guadalupe Mountains National Park, Texas* lists several endangered animal species as well as black bears, bobcats, mountain lions, and coyotes.

The Texas State Historical Association states: "The rugged terrain and isolated location of the Guadalupes kept them free from white exploration for centuries" until the middle of the nineteenth century. In the distant past "Shasta ground sloth, saber-toothed tigers, North American Rhinoceros, and mammoth roamed the Guadalupes."[159]

A 1934 article published by *Bulletin of the Texas Archeological and Paleontological Society* stated that at that time it was easier to find an elephant [mammoth] skull in Texas than that of a buffalo.[160] The author stated that some were convinced that mammoths and men coexisted. See *Secret Maps of the Ancient World* for a discussion of examples of elephants in new world art.[161] Dr. Ruskamp displays the ancient Chinese pictogram for elephant (xiang) among the Chinese writings he has identified in North America.[162]

E. Breck Parkman, Senior State Archaeologist for California State Parks wrote an interesting article identifying a few rubbing rocks of now extinct mega fauna such as mammoths. Those boulders are worn smooth on at least one side from the rubbing of

11 – Guadalupe Mountains, Texas

the animal backs against the rock.[163] That essay discusses one of those rubbing rocks at Hueco Tanks which is in the Trans-Pecos region near El Paso. The description of another archeological site in that area, which mentions a similar smooth surface of a huge rock, makes me wonder whether there might be even more rubbing rocks in that vicinity.

Elephant Rock, Shaftner, Texas

There is much rock art in the Trans-Pecos region. Some is geometric (circles, squares, triangles, etc.) and others anthropomorphic (applying human like characteristics to animals).

According to Dr. Paul Shao's *The Origin of Ancient American Cultures*, both geometric and anthropomorphic figures were also found in very early Asian art. Shao contends that examples of art of every Chinese dynasty from Shang forward are found in the Americas. Some of the art in this area of Texas appears to be maps or star charts.

In 1938 A.T. Jackson documented the unique Lobo Valley petroglyph site in Culberson County in *Picture-Writing of Texas Indians (University of Texas Anthropological Papers).*[164] The Lobo Valley is between the Van Horn Mountains and the western side of the Davis Mountains, our next stop on this journey. Numerous red boulders there are covered with elaborately carved designs.

Texas State Historical Association wrote concerning Lobo Valley:

> The site is important for the number of petroglyphs present on the boulders, for the antiquity of the carvings, and for the high contrast between the petroglyphs and the rocks upon which they are carved.[165]

Picture-Writing of Texas Indians documents petroglyphs and pictographs (painted stone) at many different sites. Those locations are not spread across the state but are predominantly in the Trans-Pecos region and are either on or not far from where Mertz charted the *Shan Hai Jing* travels.

Though I am certainly not an expert in Chinese writing, with A.T. Jackson's book in one hand and Frank Chalfant's chart[166] of examples of early Chinese characters in the other, it seems to me that several of the examples shown by Jackson may be ancient Chinese writing. I would love to see an expert check these.

Before Hendon and I were aware of research about mammoths in the Trans-Pecos area, we both thought a few times that perhaps we were seeing elephant shapes in various rock formations in that region. Later we discovered that others had written

11 – Guadalupe Mountains, Texas

about similar impressions and even named a rock in nearby Shaftner "elephant rock." Perhaps what we saw was all natural formations. However, if you go, keep your eyes and ears open for elephant shapes or names.

12 – Baldy Peak on Mt. Livermore, Texas

And it says that, three hundred li to the south, **T'AI (Bald) Mountain** is found. [Then the mountain was called the Eastern YOH or T'AI-TSUNG, which is now called T'AI Mountain. It is in the northwestern part of FUNG-KAO district, and the distance from the foot of the mountain to its summit is forty-eight li and three hundred paces.] Upon this there are **many gems,** and below it there is **much gold. Wild animals** are found here which **look like suckling pigs, but they have pearls**. They are called **TUNG-TUNG**, their name being given them in imitation of their cry. The **HWAN River** is found here, a stream **flowing easterly** into a river (or into the river, i.e. the YANG-TSZ' River). [One authority says that it flows into the sea.] In this there are many water–gems **(quartz crystals)**. (Vining translation of *Shan Hai Jing*)

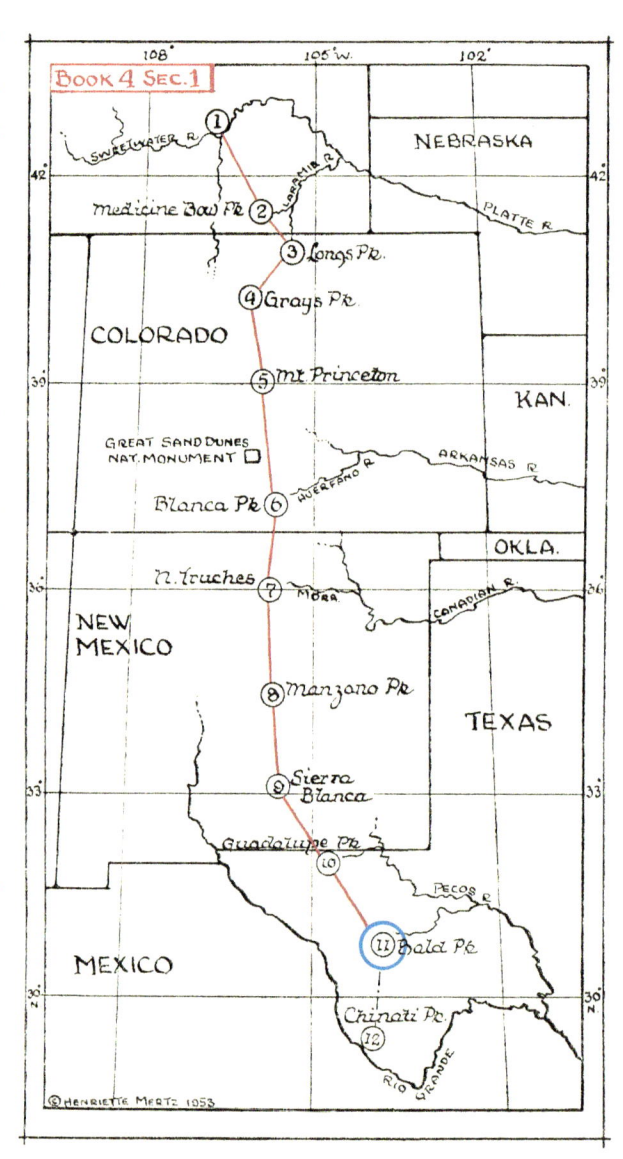

Mertz Note:

> Exactly 100 miles south, in the Davis Range, stands Bald Peak – and called "Bald Mountain" by the Chinese, an unusually pointed coincidence. The animals with pearls, are undoubtedly small peccary with tusks. The stream that flows easterly into a river, is the Coyanosa Draw, which flows east into the Pecos. Quartz of countless varieties is present.

Author's Comments:

The Chinese called this **Bald Mountain**. Ironically this is now known as Baldy Peak which sits atop Mt. Livermore in Jeff Davis County, Texas. Mt. Livermore rises straight up from the desert floor to the west.

Baldy Peak is in a huge nature conservancy with access only by permission. Between what The Nature Conservancy owns and its conservation easements on adjoining properties, almost 100,000 acres in the Davis Mountains are protected.[167]

We were told that fewer than 100 people a year enter this area because of the limited access and remote location. In contrast over 2000 people per year climb Mt. Everest.

Collared peccary courtesy of NPS

The *Shan Hai Jing* says that the **stream here flows easterly**, which it does. It also describes an animal here which they called **TUNG-TUNG that looks like a suckling pig with pearls**. Again, the *Shan Hai Jing* has identified another animal native to the Americas in its correct location.

These are collared peccary (tayassu tajacu), also known as javelina. Hendon and I saw several in this area. According to the Smithsonian they are the only native, wild, pig-like animal found in the United States.[168] Today peccary are found in New Mexico, Arizona, and the deserts of southwest Texas. Full grown they typically weigh 35 to 60 pounds.

Just as the Chinese described them, they look like cute miniature pigs with a white pearl on each side of their mouths. The "pearls" are tips of dagger-like tusks. According to Texas Tech University, normally peccary are harmless to humans and feed on various cacti. However, if threatened, they use their tusks in defense.

The *Shan Hai Jing* describes **gems** here. Agates and japers found in this area are highly prized by collectors worldwide. There is a 3000 acre ranch near Baldy Peak where for a pittance one can hunt agates. Of course, the gem hunters also need to watch for rattlesnakes.

A report by the University of Texas at Austin titled "Texas Gemstones" also lists turquoise, colorless **quartz** crystals, and sanidine as other gems found in Jeff Davis County. The *Shan Hai Jing* correctly assessed that several of these are crystals or types of **quartz**.[169]

And then the Chinese describe **gold**. Gold has been found in this area by those panning for gold. There is no recent record of gold mining in this area. However, my brother and I believe we may know where the Chinese gold mine was located. The addendum at the end of this book discusses that.

In a cave "in the shadow of Mt. Livermore," carbon dated to 1700 BC, is what is believed to be the remains of a man made shelter.[170]

In this area there were once thousands of art objects – generally small enough to hold in one's hand. Among items found here were painted bone, carved and incised bone, clay figurines, painted and incised pebbles, and carved gourds.

Miriam A. Lowrance wrote for the El Paso Archaeological Society:

> Mrs. Sarah M. Janes lived in Fort Davis in the 1890's, and much of her time was spent in collecting Indian artifacts….The collection of 1250 artifacts was donated in 1929 by Mrs. Janes to the West Texas Historical and Scientific Society, and is now in the Museum of the Big Bend on the campus of Sul Ross State University, Alpine, Texas.[171]

Lowrance then quoted *Alpine Avalanche*, April 1, 1932:

> "Mrs. Janes made seven trips up Mount Livermore in order to secure these specimens of Indian days. She rode horseback a part of the way up the mountain and crawled on her hands and knees up the most dangerous and steepest part of the mountain."[172]

Just to the south of the Trans-Pecos region of Texas, is Cueva Pilote, Mexico, another cave with some unusual objects. Altogether a minimum of 18 painted deer scapulae (shoulder blades) – several broken, some burned – were recovered from this site. Another deer scapula from another nearby Texas cave was mentioned in A. T. Jackson's *Picture Writing of the Texas Indians*. People from Cueva Pilote had contact with those in the Trans-Pecos region.[173]

History of Cartography reports that in 2000 BC Chinese made maps on copper or bronze vases.[174] Ancient Chinese, when not writing on bronze, wrote on turtle shells or cattle scapulae then burned them as oracle bones for divination. Like the Chinese oracle bones, some believe that these North American scapulae were possibly also used for divination or worship.

Note that the rock appears to be cut

Some of the rock on Baldy Peak definitely looks like it was cut or chiseled by someone at some time. There is an unusual abundance of rock art in the Trans-Pecos region including some etched onto rock, some painted. At one location is an arrangement of painted boulders which depict paired dancers. Some of the stone art in this region is so large that researchers made mosaics of photos taken from the sky (Hudspeth County) or use kite aerial photography (Reeves County) to capture each depiction.[175]

Boulder on the left, near top of knoll, appears to be hollowed out like a parapet

The El Paso Archaeological Society, Inc. produces a journal titled *The Artifact*. Two entire issues in 1987 reproduced the rock art of Jeff Davis County where Baldy Peak is found. Presidio County (our next stop on this *Shan Hai Jing* journey) also has so much rock art that in 1988 two issues were devoted to that. It is believed that the individual works of art span a very long period of time.[176]

Of course, long ago this area was not divided into counties. Brewster, Hudspeth, and Reeves Counties, which are all also in the Trans-Pecos region and border the three counties we list in reference to the *Shan Hai Jing*, each also has its own remarkable rock art and artifacts.

Ft. Davis was once the site of an Indian camp. In 1854 it was established as a fort to protect settlers from Indians. It was named after Jefferson Davis, then the US Secretary of War. Later during the War Between the States (US Civil War) Davis became president of the confederacy. Texas supported states rights and thus the confederacy.

In 1866, following the Civil War, Congress increased the number of troops. For the first time in US history black men served in the peacetime army, but were still segregated. The Ninth United States Cavalry, mainly composed of black soldiers, was sent to serve at Ft. Davis from 1867 to 1885 to continue to protect the settlers from Indian attacks.

The Indians nicknamed them "Buffalo Soldiers" because of their dark skin, curly hair, and fierce fighting spirit. The Buffalo Soldiers adopted that name with pride and even put a buffalo on their regimental crest. During that time Ft. Davis became the "most important town in the Trans-Pecos country" because it was protected and was at a crossroads of two important trails.

Originally part of Presidio County, Jeff Davis County was established in 1887 as the result of an act of the Texas legislature (apparently still supporting their confederate hero, even after the end of the war). At that time Ft. Davis was designated as the county seat. By the early 1890's the army abandoned the fort, but the town continued.

One can still take a tour of the fort which sits beside the town, just south of the Davis Mountains. In the vicinity of Ft. Davis are numerous large stones which appear to be standing on end, like those of Stonehenge. These are said to be volcanic tuff.

Volcanic tuff near Ft. Davis - photo courtesy of NPS

Hendon and I commented to each other that some of the local school children that we observed in that area looked Asian. The 2010 US Census listed no Asians and a total population of 1201 for Ft. Davis. Jeff Davis County had a total population of 2342 in 2010 or one person per square mile.

In 2009 on our second visit to study this area of Texas, my brother and I slept in bunks at a rustic building on the conservancy. In the night we heard several coyotes howling right outside. Bears had been seen there a couple of days earlier. Mountain lions, 600 pound wild boars with tusks, and rattlesnakes inhabit this region. The boars are not native and we saw huge cages set to catch them. We were told that after the boars are caught, they are shot and the carcasses dragged out of the trap. By the next morning not even their bones are left.

We were warned that because of our remote location our cell phones would not work until we reached the mountain top. Our guide, Pam, was quiet, but is a self-confident Texan. In a pendant on her necklace she wears a tiny shard of human bone that she found at a site, not far away, where her fiancé died in a small plane crash. This part of Texas is her total universe and she is content with that.

Driving for over an hour within the conservancy, we slowly ascended winding washed out roads in an open jeep. Three coyotes, as large as wolves, sauntered across the road as if they owned it. They looked our way as they

"Hendiana" Jones & the Lost Raider of the Park, starring Harris Son's Ford (OK, it's only a Jeep)

crossed, but did not seem at all fearful of us. We stopped till they passed. We also saw deer and wild turkeys along the way.

Finally the jeep could not drive any higher. The last one and a half steep miles we had to ascend on our own.

Both my brother and I were once competitive runners and we still exercise regularly. Hendon was Junior Cross Country Champion twice for the colony of Hong Kong. When we were young teens, Hendon and I took turns riding a unicycle that we co-owned.

In the 1960s in tropical Hong Kong we and our siblings swam and kayaked in a bay, hiked in the mountains, and rode bikes in the New Territories. In 1984 I was one of those who ran and carried the Olympic torch on a leg of its cross country journey to Los Angeles. In 2009 in Texas we were following another youthful adventure, but our bodies, now years later, were not as eager to obey. The air seemed thin at the high altitude. It was very windy, and numerous rocks in our path were unstable.

Pam warned us that anyone who goes up this mountain must be able to return on his own power. If a medical emergency arose we should not expect a helicopter rescue. Sudden down drafts make helicopter rescues here too risky. My brother and I took note to allow plenty of time to descend the mountain before dark. We wondered if we tarried too long, whether even our bones would be eaten like those of the slaughtered boars.

View from Mt. Livermore

Chinese were watching the stars from very early dates. If the Chinese chose this spot in Texas to observe stars, they chose well because this is one of the best star gazing areas in North America. The Milky Way (which both the Chinese and Native Americans call the "River of Heaven") is clearly visible from there.

McDonald Observatory is on an adjacent mountain. Some originally wanted to put the observatory on Baldy Peak, but access was too difficult.

I can attest that access to Baldy Peak is not easy. The top is over 8300 ft. (2500 meters) in elevation. To reach the summit our guide instructed us how to crawl up the last several yards – straight up rocks that in warm weather rattlesnakes use for sunning. Though it was a cloudy day, from the top my brother and I saw the adjacent stops named by the Chinese to the north and to the south.

View from Mt. Livermore

However, the *Shan Hai Jing*'s mention that the mountain 300 li to the south was "Bamboo Mountain," stopped me in my tracks. Looking south I saw mile after mile of the Chihuahuan Desert. Bamboo needs water. I doubted that bamboo could possibly grow in dry West Texas.

Thinking that surely this reference to bamboo would prove the *Shan Hai Jing* wrong, the next day we visited the local museum to ask whether there is anything in Texas that looks like bamboo.

"Yes, river cane."

"Where?"

"By Chinati Peak." (Where Mertz placed it.)

12 – Baldy Peak on Mt. Livermore, Texas

However, local archeologists would not even discuss with us the possibility that early Chinese may have been in Texas. The only Chinese they would discuss were the ones who built the railroad in the nineteenth century.

Unusual rock formations in the Davis Mountains

13 – Chinati Peak, Texas

And it says that, three hundred li to the south, **Bamboo Mountain** is found, bordering on a river (or the river). [One authority says that it is on the shore-or that it is at the **boundary-line**.] There is **no grass or trees**, but there are many **green jasper and green-jade stones**. The **KIH River** (or water **impeded** in its course **by rocks**) is found here, a **stream flowing southeasterly into the TS'U-TAN River** (or body of water). In this (country) there is a great abundance of **dye-plants**.

The first section of the "Classic of the Eastern Mountains" thus gives the entire distance along the twelve mountains, from SUH-CHU Mountain to Bamboo Mountain, as three thousand six hundred li. Their **gods all have human bodies and dragons' heads**. When they are offered a **sacrifice of** animals having hair, a **dog** is used. In other sacrifices the **blood** of a fish is used to besmear the things offered. [To use blood in besmearing the thing offered in sacrifice is called 'NI.' KUNG-YANG'S 'Chronicles' say that in offering sacrifices of creatures having flesh and blood, to the god of the land, and of grain, they besmear with blood the being that is sacrificed. The name of this species of sacrifice is pronounced 'NI.'] (Vining translation of *Shan Hai Jing*)

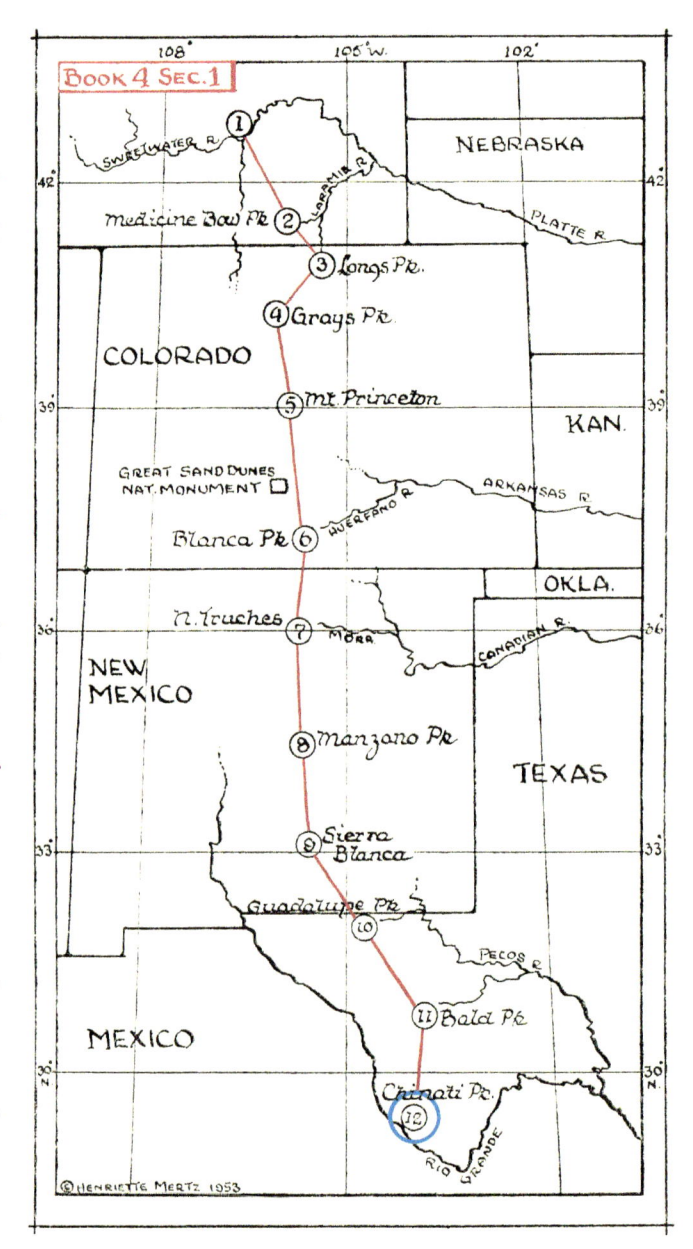

- 120 -

13 – Chinati Peak, Texas

Mertz Note:

This last peak named could either be Emory Peak or Chinati Peak, both on the Rio Grande. Although Emory Peak is 100 miles south and Chinati only 85 miles, it is believed that, of the two, Chinati fits the description. Not too far away, the river is impeded in it course – near the little town of Ruidoso (noisy) – and the Rio Grande flows southeast, while it bends around Emory Peak. The ancient Chinese scholar who examined this account added that from the description it appeared that the river formed a boundary line – and so it does now, interestingly enough. The large body of water, recorded by the Chinese, is the Gulf of Mexico into which the Rio Grande empties.

The Chinese computation of 1200 miles figures approximately 100 miles more, as the crow flies, than my map indicates. However, that distance is compensated for in the area from Medicine Bow Peak to Blanca Peak, where the circuitous route threads through half a dozen insurmountably high mountain passes. In measuring distance by stepping off paces, the Chinese would have inevitably have had to have travelled a greater distance on foot than a pair of dividers measures that distance on a flat paper map. On level stretches, the tabulation is within a mile or two of being accurate – a most astounding feat for anyone at any time in that country. The general path has followed longitude 106 W., with comparatively little variation from 43° N. to 30° N.

Author's Comments:

Today the highway called the Texas Mountain Trail connects Guadalupe Peak to Presidio through the towns of Van Horn and Marfa, a town a short distance from Baldy Peak.[177] Therefore, this connects the last three stops on this *Shan Hai Jing* journey.

Further connection of the last three *Shan Hai Jing* locations is mentioned by archeologist A.T. Jackson in quoting Garrick Mallery's 1889 account of a very old map scratched on the back of a boulder in the Van Horn Mountains. The map depicted a nearby Indian trail and indicated locations of water sources along the route. That trail started on the Rio Grande just north of Chinati Peak, passed through the Van Horn Mountains to the Davis Mountains, from there to the southern end of the Guadalupe Mountains, and then north into New Mexico.[178]

A report for the Texas Archeological Society states that at ancient quarries near Van Horn are:

> enormous quantities of varied lithic materials – cherts, agates, and felsites. The presence of numerous quarry sites attests to the fact that prehistoric people made heavy use of the area.
>
> Dr. Joe Ben Wheat discovered a large Paleo-Indian site near Van Horn which led him to believe that "Wild Horse Creek drainage system was part of an easy and well-traveled route into the Rio Grande country."[179]

Arundinaria gigantean - photo courtesy of bamboogarden.com

Chinati Peak in Presidio County, Texas, is found at the location the Chinese called **Bamboo Mountain**. As previously mentioned, native river cane (arundinaria gigantean), which looks like Asian bamboo, grew wild near there by the river.

River cane, now close to extinction because of clearing for farming and livestock, had many uses for Native Americans. They made arrows from it, used it for roofing material in adobe houses, and even ate the shoots – as Asians eat bamboo shoots.

The web site USDA Plants shows river cane in Texas, but not currently at this location. However, there are photos on the internet posted by academic studies which show

13 – Chinati Peak, Texas

it there in the recent past.[180] According to the National Park Service, arundinaria gigantean is the only species of bamboo native to the US.

The top of Chinati Peak at 7728 feet is dry and desolate and has **no grass and no trees**. Except for the river and the Chinati Mountains, it is surrounded by the Chihuahuan Desert. In the Apache language Chinati means "black birds."[181] Some rocks near the top of Chinati Peak have an azure hue so the mountains are also sometimes called "the mountains of the Blue Rock."[182]

Chinati Mountains courtesy of Creative Commons

The *Shan Hai Jing* says that here the **KIH river is impeded by rocks**. This river is known today as the Rio Grande. At the base of this mountain is a hamlet named Ruidosa (noisy) because of the sound of the river when it hit the rocks – exactly as the Chinese mentioned. (At Sierra Blanca, New Mexico we discussed another town, Ruidoso, which is a variant spelling of the same word.) Because of drought in recent years the level of the Rio Grande now is down considerably.

The Chinese said that **this river flows south easterly into a body of water**. From this location the Rio Grande flows south then east and finally into the Gulf of Mexico.

Some of the strange customs mentioned in the *Shan Hai Jing* as practiced by the people in this area can be explained. The **gods** that **had human bodies and dragon heads** could well have either been masks worn by the Native Americans[183] or the previously mentioned anthropomorphic art, used in both China and the early Americas, in which animals take on human like characteristics. Some of the Native American **sacrifices** were indeed very **bloody**. I detailed **dog sacrifices** by Native Americans that were strikingly similar to those in Asia in *Secret Maps of the Ancient World*.[184]

Texas kidneywood (Eysenhardtia texana Scheele) is used to make **dyes**.[185] According to USDA Plants Database, this is a native plant found exclusively in a few counties in Texas including Presidio County. The natives also used the fruit of the plains prickly pear (Opuntia polyacantha Haw) to make dye. Prickly pear is found in many of the western states, but only in a few counties in Texas including Presidio.

Jasper, agate, marble, chalcedony, and fluorite are all found in the area of Chinati Peak. I could find no mention of jade anywhere in Texas.

Flourite is green as is some chalcedony, but since they are transparent or translucent, surely they would not have been mistaken for jade. However, some **green** moss agate found locally looks strikingly similar to **jade**. It is commonly found there in cobbles three to six inches in diameter and sometimes twice that size. Those gems are not easy to spot because they usually have a thin white coating, which makes them look like all the other rocks.

According to a report published by the University of Texas at Austin:

> Various amounts of agate, jasper, and chalcedony occur in the gravels of the Rio Grande….The jasper in the Rio Grande gravels is yellow, red, green, or various shades of these…[186]

That study states that good agate of various colors is found in many localities in Presidio County.

Church in Ruidosa courtesy of Thomas Rinard

Ruidosa is now a ghost town. Just downstream is the town of Presidio. The 2010 US Census lists the population of the whole county at 7818. The annual average high temperature is 87. The annual average low is 54.6 – which make ideal conditions for farming. However, average annual precipitation is only 10.8

inches a year.[187] A thin ribbon of green vegetation outlines the river. Otherwise, desert stretches for miles.

The Mexican river, Rio Conchos, which reportedly carries even more water than the Rio Grande, merges with the Rio Grande at Presidio. Texas and Beyond, a virtual museum of Texas Cultural Heritage presented by the University of Texas at Austin, groups the towns of Ruidosa and Presidio together with a small adjacent portion of Mexico as three prongs to form "La Junta de los Rios District" or "La Junta" for short – a junction of fertile river valleys with life giving waters capable of growing crops.

Texas State Historical Association wrote concerning Presidio:

> The surrounding area is the oldest continuously cultivated area in the United States. Farmers have lived at Presidio since 1500 B.C.…The first Spaniards came to Presidio in 1535 when Alvar Nunez Cabeza de Vaca and his three companions stopped at the Indian Pueblo, placed a cross on the mountain side, and called the village La Junta de las Cruces.[188]

In line with the idea of La Junta being a community, Cabeza de Vaca stated that in 1535 the people living along the river spoke the same language. He regarded them as the best looking natives he had seen and considered them the most healthy and energetic.

The other Native American groups that Cabeza de Vaca previously encountered traveled from location to location as hunter-gatherers. These people in La Junta were the first natives he met while traveling for several years through the American southwest who cultivated crops. Here they grew beans, squash, and corn.

Earlier Cabeza de Vaca saw people with cotton garments, but he did not know the source of it. He wrote that the people in the La Junta area mentioned other tribes which had cotton blankets. By having something made of cotton, they were either growing cotton or trading with someone who did.

I have not been able to verify what date cotton plants reached Texas. However, *Prehistoric New Mexico, Background for Survey,* indicates that it was common among the Mogollon in New Mexico by AD 100 - 300.[189] Dr. Ruth Shady Solis reported cotton in Peru that carbon dated to around 2000 BC.[190]

Cotton native to the Americas cannot be made into cloth unless it is cross bred with old world cotton. American cotton spun into cloth has chromosomes from both old and new world. Therefore, any cotton used in the Americas to make cloth is a cultigen.

China had cotton at very early dates. Dr. John Sorenson and Dr. Carl Johannessen wrote:

> The early history of cotton (Gossypium spp.) in the New World is found, on the basis of cytogenetic analysis, to be tied directly to Asian cotton.[191]

The presence of cotton blankets in the La Junta vicinity indicates that the people there had either direct or indirect contact with Asians at some time period before the arrival of the Spaniards.

In 1582 when more Spaniards reached this area, their report contended that the people to the south of this area spoke a different language than those in La Junta. The 1582 report estimated that at that time over 10,000 people were living there.

Texas Beyond History mentions competing hypotheses to explain the origins of village life in La Junta – colonization vs. indigenous development.[192] Texas Beyond History asks:

> How did this cultural crossroad come to be in the first place? When did settled life begin at La Junta? Who were the first villagers?[193]

In my opinion pottery shards from that area look similar to early incised Asian pottery.

According to El Paso Archaeological Society many different sites of rock art are found in Presidio County.[194] The oldest is thought to be from around 2000 BC or prior.

There is evidence of previous flooding by the Rio Grande. Archeologists suspect that some of the oldest items of the La Junta region probably were destroyed by those deluges. Few ancient artifacts were found right by the river in contrast to numerous archaic items in locations not far away.

> Late Archaic sites are found in practically every ecological niche in the region, from the lowest basins to the highest mountain peaks. The sites from this period are accompanied by a wide variety of dart point types.[195]

Ceremonial Cave is further north in Hudspeth County. It is in the Hueco Mountains east of El Paso. Offerings there are thought to have begun 2000 years ago or earlier. Although this location is hundreds of miles inland, several items which originated on the Pacific Ocean were found there including Olivella shell beads, abalone pendant from the Pacific, mother of pearl from Pacific coast abalone shells, beads made from shell of vermetid snail, and a bracelet cut from the shell of Glycymeris (a marine mollusk of the Pacific Coast).[196]

According to expert Miriam Lowrance, some of the rock art of this region shows signs that it was painted over or reworked at different times.[197] However, in 2009 at a Texas university when I suggested to an archeologist that I thought that perhaps I was seeing Chinese writing etched beneath the painting in the photo of rock art that she was showing me, she became angry and abruptly ended my session with her. Could some of the currently prized rock art actually just be old graffiti over ancient etchings?

Photo by and courtesy of © Gary Nafis

Although the comment in the *Shan Hai Jing* about the river being a boundary is in parentheses and thus was inserted later than the original text, this stretch of the Rio Grande near Presidio is a natural **boundary line** between the USA and Mexico. My brother Hendon and I did not go up to the border because of occasional political unrest in border towns the past few years. We do not recommend at this time that others go right up to the border either. Hendon and I viewed Chinati Peak from a nearby road.

This was our last stop on this particular *Shan Hai Jing* journey. Of the *Shan Hai Jing* travelers, some had to go back to China to give the report. Did some of the travel weary Chinese stay in this area? Were they the earliest inhabitants?

14 – Conclusions

In addition to correctly telling how the rivers flowed, what the mountains looked like, and which minerals were in each location, this *Shan Hai Jing* journey correctly placed the following, which are native to North America:

Chapter 2 Near Casper, WY
- Pronghorn

Chapter 3 Medicine Bow Peak, WY
- Wyoming Toads

Chapter 4 Longs Peak, CO
- Dusky grouse
- Razorback sucker fish

Chapter 6 Mount Princeton, CO
- Yellowfin Cutthroat Trout

Chapter 7 Blanca Peak, CO
- Rocky Mountain White Oak

Chapter 10 Sierra Blanca, New Mexico
- Gray Wolf
- Yellow bellied marmot

Chapter 11 Guadalupe Mountains. TX
- Horned lizard

Chapter 12 Baldy Peak, TX
- Peccary

Chapter 13 Chinati Peak, TX
- River cane
- Dye plants

In addition, the Chinese correctly named two locations where plants of Chinese origin (white mulberry and ailanthus) are found. What are the odds of someone across the Pacific who had never been to North America being able to do that? How can one explain the Chinese writing and all the Asian customs practiced by Native American tribes?

So if this trip was real, when was it?

- It had to have been sometime after the start of the first Chinese dynasty and before Chao-shi wrote about the *Shan Hai Jing* sometime before 9 AD.
- Since we find Chinese writing on the route, one would presume that the trip was after writing was invented in China.
- It was after Chinese were cultivating crops.
- It was while wolves were still at Sierra Blanca.
- If the Chinese on this expedition brought Setaria viridis to Manzano Peak one would presume that the trip was before millet was widely used in China and before maize replaced Setaria viridis as a staple to Native Americans.
- If this expedition was involved in the transport of the peanut to China, that happened before 2000 BC.
- If the McKean Complex was actually Chinese, that has already been dated to 2000 BC.
- I believe that he petroglyphs holding the names of early Chinese kings validates journeys after the *Shan Hai Jing* journey.

My research only involves America and China. However, the *Shan Hai Jing* claimed journeys around the world. If the Chinese really did make it to North America at early dates, then all of world history should be re-examined. All those ancient *Shan Hai Jing* journeys could have been done using ocean currents that surround the globe.

Shang Civilization published by Yale University Press shows photos of Negroid, Caucasoid, and Eskimoid skulls unexplainably found in ancient Chinese graves.[198] Did Chinese go to those regions and then take back slaves? The *Shan Hai Jing*, in discussion of another part of the world, mentions hippopotami, which one might assume would further imply that they went to Africa.

Furthermore, the style of ancient rock art found in the Big Horn Basin, Wyoming mentioned in Chapter 1 is not only been linked to Ningxia, China but reportedly also was found in Namibia, Africa and in Alta, Norway and other locations around the world. Someone took it to those places. If not the Chinese, then who?

My friend Cedric Bell of the United Kingdom is doing research and has written a book (as of this writing not yet published) about evidences of ancient Chinese in the British Isles about the time of the Roman occupation of that area.

Please return with me to the round Chinese star charts with 28 spokes which I mentioned at the start of this book.

We all know that Stonehenge in the UK indicates equinoxes and solstices. Recently when viewing an aerial shot of Stonehenge, I noticed that the part of Stonehenge that we see in photos (the upright rocks with the mantles connecting them) is only the hub of a wheel. Outside of that, cut as a ditch into the ground, is another larger circle about 330 feet (100 meters) in diameter. Just inside the earthen bank to the ditch is a circle with 56 postholes.[199] Is it possible that at one time at Stonehenge, those 56 posts were holding in position 28 spokes to the hub and that this was another Chinese astronomical device?

Dr. Christopher L.C.E. Witcombe wrote concerning the 56 holes: "Archaeological investigations have shown that these holes were not dug to hold upright stones or wooden posts."[200] Although the postholes are evenly spaced, he contends that the 28 day cycle of the moon can be tracked with those posts.

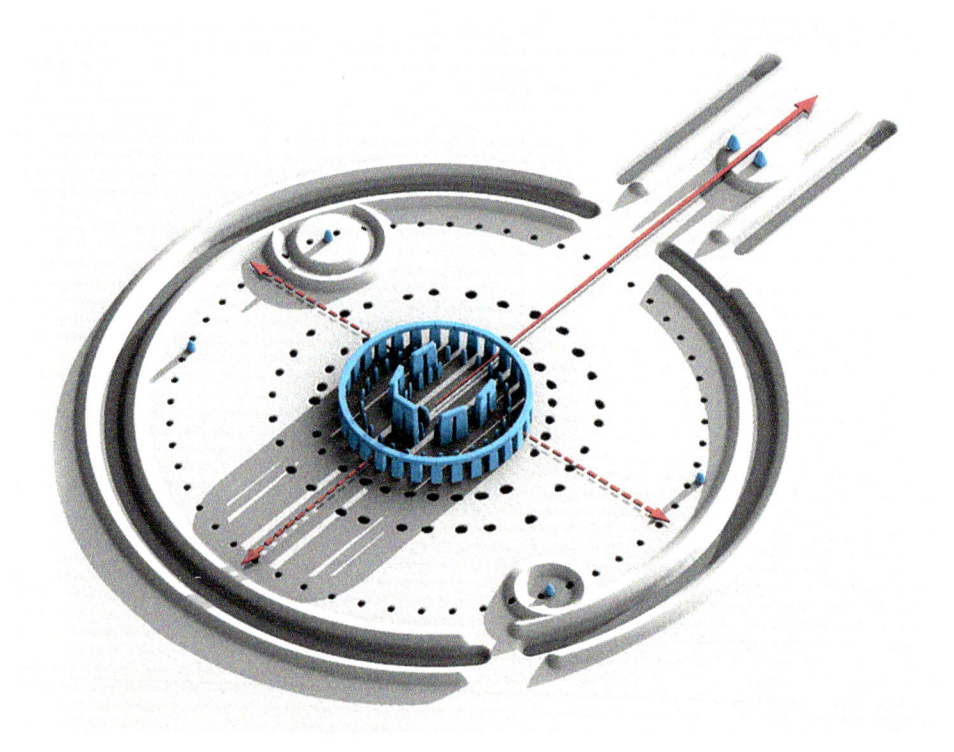

Computer rendering of Stonehenge courtesy of Jlert Joseph Lertola

In *The Asiatic Fathers of America* my father expressed the desire that other researchers would "pick up the spade and dig deeper." That is my sentiment as well. My abridgement of *The Asiatic Fathers of America* (148 pages) only covers a small part of what my father actually wrote (almost 800 pages). His original book needs to be studied in depth by serious scholars.

14 – Conclusions

The History of Cartography, which the Library of Congress told me was the "Bible" on maps, states that over seventy two percent of the place names on world maps of the ch'onhado (tian xia) style are from the *Shan Hai Jing*. (That is the type of world map found in the *Dr. Hendon M. Harris, Jr. Map Collection*. This is the world map that started my father, then me many years later, on this quest.)

The History of Cartography confirms the: "general congruence of directional relationship between the *Shanhai Jing* and the ch'onhado."[201] Therefore, perhaps by using both the *Shan Hai Jing* and these world maps, the whole world can be re-examined in a new light.

For hundreds of years people have debated about whether the *Shan Hai Jing* was truth or fiction. Some have prejudices against re-examining history in that light. Some even have a vested interest – ethnic, religious, or academic – that the *Shan Hai Jing* be untrue.

There are numerous separate accounts in recent years of petroglyphs or ancient art purposely defaced, destroyed, or lost. The early Spanish priests purposely destroyed Native American writings, believing that they were of the devil. In *A Critical Reprise of 'Aboriginal' American History*, Dr. Covey stated: "U. Michigan destroyed over 5,000 inscribed tablets and figurines dug from Hopewill mounds in the Detroit area 1890-1920, assuming fakes on the premise that nobody in America could have been literate before Columbus."[202]

In *Secret Maps of the Ancient World* I cited four pages of examples in which evidence of early visitors to America was purposely destroyed or defaced.[203] I have since learned of even more documented instances.

In one case, clay tablets with writing on them found in a cave in Texas in the 1960s were turned in to a park ranger. Some clay tablets in museums are over 4000 years old. However, later when someone asked to view those Texas tablets they were no longer there. One account was that they lay on the floor of a maintenance shed for months. The tablets were moved around the shed until they disintegrated.

Some institutions do not properly protect artifacts. Others conceal information by ignoring or refusing to discuss it. The longer we wait, the more evidence will be gone forever. **Secrets exist when information is withheld or clues are ignored.**

Addendum - Where Was the Baldy Peak Gold Mine?

It is believed that Chinese gold mining in early times was by sluicing, which is a process of washing liquids over minerals through a sluice box. The gravels (tailings), which weigh less, are washed away and the heavier gold is left.

Before we even went to this area of Texas, both Hendon and I thought that on Google Maps we could see evidences of strip mining or disturbed soil near the top of Mt. Livermore. An indention near the top of Mt. Livermore looks very much like a caldera.

Hendon inquired at a local university, but was told that there is no record of strip mining in that area. He was also told that there is much indication of volcanic activity, but no calderas there either.

The bowl is shaped like a caldera. This photo was shot from west of Baldy Peak looking east.

Pam, our guide, pointed out that if one views Mt. Livermore on Google Earth and turns the north on the top circle to the bottom (south is then at the top) that he can see the area clearer. Using this method, Hendon contends that the basin that looks like a caldera was the sluice. He points out that there is a stream and tailings coming out of the small opening on the western side of that basin.

The walls and interior basin is lighter and thus stand out on Google Maps. Miriam Lowrance, who wrote about the rock art in the area commented: "The Mount Livermore area is a region of massive broken terrain…"[204] Why would people at any time period break up stone in a massive way high on a mountain?

Hendon states that he believes that disturbance of the ground, and possibly also bleaching, highlighted this area. One of the processes used today to remove gold involves bleaching. However, we have not been able to locate any documentation that bleaching was used by Chinese in ancient times.

Hendon pointed out to me several excerpts from a rare book he acquired, *The History of the Former Han Dynasty* Vol. III by Pan Ku, which in 1955 was translated from Chinese to English by the widely acclaimed sinologist, Dr. Homer H. Dubs. The Former Han Dynasty lasted from 202 BC through AD 9.[205]

This text contains several interesting statements. One was by court courier Wang Mang, who later became ruler himself. In speaking to the Empress Dowager, Wang reminded her:

> the Huangchih [came] from [a distance of] thirty thousand li to offer a live rhinoceros as tribute.

When referring to rhinos most people think of Africa, which perhaps is where that one came from. The text goes on:

> Kings of the Eastern Barbarians crossed the Great Ocean to offer the treasures of their states…[206]

In this same conversation Wang referred to the Eastern Sea, the Southern Sea and the Northern Sea. Who were those "Eastern Barbarians" across the "Great Ocean"? Could they have come from the Americas?

In the appendix Dubs commented on the text. Dubs told that when Wang Mang was ruler, he enacted a plan in which it became illegal for individuals in China to own gold. They all had to turn gold in to the government in exchange for cash. According to the official records, at that time there was about 5,000,000 troy ounces of gold in China. Between 135BC and AD 23 the amount of gold in China had tripled.

Dubs stated that the gold of all of Europe in the middle ages was only 3,750,000 ounces. No large amounts of gold had been mined in China at any time up to then. The question arose: "From where did all that new gold in China come?" Dubs concluded that it had come from outside of China through trade or mining.[207] Perhaps some of it even originated in the Americas.

Surely if the Chinese explorers found gold, they would have taken what they mined. If gold was mined there, evidence should still exist in the tailings. It is said that the best place today to find gold is where it was found before. In 2010 a man found a 100 ounce gold nugget in California in the vicinity of previous mining.[208]

Not far from Baldy Peak is a petroglyph that appears to be a map, I do not know the significance it. It may or may not have something to do with the location of the mine or the gold.

If you would like to see a sketch of that petroglyph, please contact me through my website www.AsiaticFathers.com. Through the "Contact" icon there, under "Remarks," ask for "Sketch of petroglyph near Baldy Peak" and it will be sent to you at no charge as an e-mail attachment.

About The Author

Charlotte Harris Rees has appeared on television and National Public Radio in the United States and Canada and in numerous international news articles about her family's map collection and her research concerning the very early arrival of Chinese to America.

She has given many presentations including at the Library of Congress (Washington, DC); The National Library of China (Beijing); Stanford University; the University of London; Tsinghua University (Beijing); University of British Columbia; Zheng He Symposium (Melaka, Malaysia); Switzerland; the University of Maryland; City University of New York; Seton Hall University; the Chinese Historical Society (Los Angeles); and the Royal Geographical Society (London and Hong Kong).

In 1972 her father, Dr. Hendon Harris, Jr. (1916-1981), found in an antique shop in Korea an ancient Asian map which led him to write a book of almost 800 pages. That text contended that by 2200 B.C. Chinese had reached the Americas by sea.

Since early 2003, Rees, an independent researcher, a retired federal employee, and an honors graduate of Columbia International University, has diligently studied the possibility of very early arrival of Chinese to America. Her mentor, Dr. Cyclone Covey, has researched this China/America connection for 60 years.

In 2003 Rees and her brother took the Harris Map Collection to the Library of Congress where it remained for three years while being studied. In 2006 she published an abridged version of her father's, *The Asiatic Fathers of America: Chinese Discovery and Colonization of Ancient America*. Her *Secret Maps of the Ancient World* came out in 2008. In late 2011 she released *Chinese Sailed to America Before Columbus: More Secrets from the Dr. Hendon M. Harris, Jr. Map Collection*. Her books are listed by World Confederation of Institutes and Libraries for Chinese Overseas Studies. This is her first travelogue.

Her father, Dr. Harris, a third generation Baptist missionary, was born in Kaifeng, China. As a child Rees lived for four years in Taiwan then later for a year in Hong Kong. In recent years she has taken several trips to China. Her home is in Virginia.

Acknowledgements

Photos in this book were shot by Dave or Charlotte Rees unless otherwise noted. Two maps of rivers and the map of the Continental Divide Trail are by Dave.

Writing a book requires the assistance of many people and I appreciate all who helped me. Their mention below does not imply that they endorse my findings.

I would like to thank the following:

Camilla Anderson, Tom Baker, Dr. Cyclone Covey, Jerry Friedman, Pamela Gaddis, Hendon Harris, III, Dr. John Hebert, Amy Hopperstad, Dr. Hwa-Wei Lee, Dr. Linda Larcombe, Jlert Joseph Lertola, Bob Meistrell, Ron Merkle, Gary Nafis, Robert Temple, Daniel Rees, Dave Rees, Thomas Rinard, Dr. John Ruskamp, Linda Ruskamp, Shang Haifeng, Wallace Turnbull, Wally Turnbull, Carol Wang (Wang Xu), Daniel Zajic, Dr. Jianping Zhang, Library of Congress, National Library of China, United States National Park Service (NPS), United States National Oceanic and Atmospheric Administration (NOAA), United States Department of Agriculture (USDA), US Fish and Wildlife Service (USFWS), US Forest Service (fs. fed.us), Geology Department, University of Wyoming; Oregon Department of Fish and Wildlife, The Nature Conservancy (Texas), Bamboogarden.com, and Torchflame Books.

Endnotes

1. Kwang-Chih Chang, *The Archaeology of Ancient China,* New Haven, CT: Yale University Press, 1972, pp. 97-99.

2. James Duguid and Gabriel Bedish, "An Analysis of the Spanish Diggings Region of Wyoming During Paleolithic Inhabitation" WyAr 11(1) 1968 Part 2 Wyoming Archaeological Society.

3. "The McKean Complex," University of Manitoba n.d. Web 4 October 2012 <http://www.umanitoba.ca/faculties/arts/anthropology/manarchnet/chronology/archaic/mckean.html>.

4. John A. Eddy, "Astronomical Alignment of the Big Horn Medicine Wheel," *Science,* 7 June 1974, Vol. 184, No. 4141, pp. 1035 – 1043.

5. "Ancient Observatories Timeless Knowledge: Bighorn Medicine Wheel" n.d. Web. 18 October 2012 <http://www.solar-center.stanford.edu/AO/bighorn.html>.

6. Robert Temple, *The Genius of China,* Rochester, Vermont: Inner Traditions: 1986, 1998, 2007, p.37-39.

7. I.S. Bartlett, ed., *History of Wyoming* Vol. I, Chicago: The S. J. Clarke Publishing Company, 1918, p. 41.

8. Edward Payson Vining, *An Inglorious Columbus: Evidence that Hwui Shan and a Party of Buddhist Monks from Afghanistan Discovered America,* London: D. Appleton and Company, 1885, p. 221.

9. Michael FitzGerald, "Portals to Other Realities," *Wall Street Journal*, 18 September 2010 Web 8 June 2013 <http://www.online.wsj.com/artile/SB10001424052748704644404575482342261278092.html>.

10. Paola Dematte, "The Rock Art of Inner Mongolia and Ningxia" n.d.Web 12 May 2013 <http://www.bradshawfoundation.com/china/ningxia/index.php>.

11. "Boulder Monuments" n.d. Web 19 October 2012 <http://www.esask.uregina.ca/tmc_cms/modules/customcode/includes/print_entry.cfm?entryid=7344226D-1560-95>.

12. Kwang-Chih Chang, *Early Chinese Civilization: Anthropological Perspectives,* Cambridge, MA: Harvard University Press, 1976, p. 45 and Chang, *The Archeology of Ancient China,* p. 157.

13. Nasir El Bassan, *Handbook of Bioenergy Crops: A Complete Reference to Species Development and Applications,* Oxford, UK: Routledge, 2010.

14. All the notes by Henriette Mertz are taken from her 1953 privately published *Pale Ink* unless otherwise noted.

15 Henriette Mertz, *Gods from the Far East: How the Chinese Discovered America*, New York: Ballantine Books, 1972, p. 132. (This note is not found in *Pale Ink).*

16 *National Historic Trails: Auto Tour Route Interpretive Guide, Across Wyoming,* Salt Lake City: National Park Service, 2007, p. 2.

17 Curtis Ebbesmeyer & Eric Scigliano, *Flotsametrics and the Floating World*, New York: Smithsonian Books, 2009, p. 158.

18 R. A. Barkley, "The Kuroshio Current," 1973 web 10 December 2012 <http://www.swfsc.noaa.gov/publications/CR/1973/7302.PDF>.

19 Rees, *Secret Maps of the Ancient World,* Bloomington, IN: Authorhouse, 2008, 2009, p. 90.

20 Joseph Needham, *Science and Civilisation in China,* Vol. 4 Physics and Physical Technology, Part 3 Civil Engineering and Nautics, Cambridge: Cambridge University Press, 1971, pp 548-549.

21 Ebbesmeyer and Scigliano, p. 140.

22 *National Historic Trails,* p. 4.

23 *National Historic Trails,* p. 18.

24 "Devil's Gate – California National Historic Trail," National Park Service n.d. Web 8 October 12 <http://www.nps.gov/cali/planyourvisit/site6.htm>.

25 "The Devil's Gate" n.d. Web 8 October 2012 < http://www.wyoshpo.state.wy.us/trailsdemo/devilsgate.htm>.

26 Bartlett, p. 43.

27 "Official Song of the State of Kansas" n.d. Web 9 October 2012 <http://www.50states.com/songs/kansas.htm#.UHR9ARV1B2A>.

28 Charlotte Harris Rees, *Chinese Sailed to America Before Columbus: More Secrets from the Dr. Hendon M. Harris, Jr. Map Collection,* Bloomington, IN: Authorhouse, 2011, p. 66.

29 "Wyoming Toad: Almost extinct in America's backyard," Amphibian Rescue and Conservation Project 15 October 2012 Web 17 November 2012 <http://www.amphibianrescue,org/tag/bufo-hemiophrys/>.

30 "State & County QuickFacts – Census Bureau" n.d. Web 11 October 2012 <http://www.quickfacts.census.gov/qfd/index.html>.

31 Michael McCoy, *Off the Beaten Path Wyoming: A Guide to Unique Places,* Guilford, CT: Globe Pequot Press, 2010, pp. 16, 27.

32 McCoy, p. 29.

33 W. Dan Hausel, *Mining History and Geology of Some of Wyoming's Metal and Gemstone Districts and Deposits,* Reprint No. 56, Laramie, WY: The Geological Survey of Wyoming, 1994, p. 42.

34 McCoy, p. 25.

35	W. Dan Hausel, *Guide to the Geology, Mining Districts and Ghost Towns of Medicine Bow and Snowy Ridge Scenic Byway*, Public Information Circular No. 32, Laramie, WY: The Geological Survey of Wyoming, 1993, p. 28.
36	Ibid.
37	National Register of Historic Places Inventory Nomination Form, Libby Lodge, Snowy Range Lodge, Sept. 30, 1976, Web 18 November 2012 <http://www.pdfhost.focus.nps.gov/docs/NRHP/Text/76001947.pdf>.
38	Bartlett, p. 37.
39	Bartlett, p. 34-36.
40	"Site of Ancient Copper Mine:Site of Ancient Copper Mine in Tongling" n.d. Web. 8 October 2012 <http://www.whc.unesco.org/en/tenativelists/5333/>.
41	Mertz, *Gods from the Far East*, p. 134.
42	"Rawah Wilderness Area" n.d. Web 14 November 2012 <http://www.coha.dri.edu/web/state_analysis/Colorado/RawahWA_metdesc.html>.
43	Mike Xu, "New Evidence for Pre-Columbian Transpacific Contact between China and Mesoamerica," *Journal of the Washington Academy of Sciences,* Vol. 88 No. 1, Mar 2002, pp 1-11.
44	A. H. Koschmann and M. H. Bergendahl, *Principal Gold-Producing Districts of the United States,* Geological Survey Professional Paper 610, Washington, DC: United States Government Printing Office, 1968, p. 85.
45	Kwang-chih Chang, *The Archaeology of Ancient China*, p. 86.
46	Richard E. Strassberg, *A Chinese Bestiary: Strange Creatures from the Guideways Through Mountains and Seas,* Berkeley: University of California Press, 2002, p. 112.
47	"Grays Peak and Torreys Peak" n.d. Web 2 January 2013 <http://www.protrails.com/trails/view/384/.../grays-peak-and-torreys-peak>.
48	E. Steve Cassells, *The Archaeology of Colorado,* Boulder, CO: Johnson Books, 1997, p.102.
49	Rees, *Secret Maps of the Ancient World,* pp. 40 – 42.
50	Cyclone Covey, *A Critical Reprise of 'Aboriginal' American History,* Winston Salem, NC: Wake Forest University, 2000-2005, p. 214.
51	Leo Bagrow, *History of Cartography,* revised and enlarged by R. A. Skelton, Cambridge: Harvard University Press, 1966, p. 197.
52	"Grays and Torreys Trail" n.d. Web 5 September 2012 <http://www.sangres.com/colorado/national-forests/arapaho/trails/graysandtorreys-54htm>.
53	John Fielder, *John Fielder's Best of Colorado,* Englewood, CO: Westcliffe Publishers, 2002, 2003, 2004, p. 59.

54 "Grays Peak – Torreys Peak" n.d. Web 2 January 2013 <http://www.cloudhiking.com/mountains/rockies/grays-torreys.php>.

55 "Continental Divide Peaks Colorado" 6 August 2012 Web 11 October 2012 <http://www.summitpost.org/continental-divide-peaks-colorado/172039>.

56 "An Amazing Past" n.d. Web 2 January 2012 <http://www.leadville.org/an-amazing-past.html>.

57 "Leadville History: 1878-1893" n.d. Web 2 January 2013 <http://www.visitleadvilleco.com/history>.

58 "An Amazing Past" n.d. Web 2 January 2012 < http://www.leadville.org/an-amazing-past.html>.

59 "Leadville Attractions" n.d. Web 2 January 2013 <http://www.visitleadvilleco.com/attractions>.

60 "Colorado Legends: Leadville-Cloud City" n.d. Web 2 January 2013 <http://www.legendsofamerica.com/co-leadville.html>.

61 *Upper Arkansas Valley Outdoor Adventure Guide*, Salida, CO: Arkansas Valley Publishing Co., 2012.

62 "Dream Stream (South Platte) – Half Day" n.d. Web 22 October 2012 <http://www.arkanglers.com/dream-stream-south-platte-half-day>.

63 Kevin Rogers, "Cutthroat Trout" n.d. Web 14 November 2012 <http://www.wildlife.state.co.us/research/aquatic/CutthroatTrout/Pages/CutthroatTrout.aspx#greenback>.

64 "Yellowfin Cutthroat Trout/Rocky Mountain Wild" n.d. Web 4 January 2013 <http://www.rockymountainwild.org/species/fish/yellowfin-cutthroat-trout>.

65 "Salmo Trutta (brown trout)" Nonindigenous Aquatic Species n.d. Web 8 November 2012 <http://www.nas.er.usgs.gov/queries/factsheet.aspx?SpeciesID=931>.

66 "The Louisiana Purchase 'Opens' the West - Other Explores Follow Lewis & Clark: Stephen H. Long" n.d. Web 22 October 2012 <http://www.nebraskastudies.org/0400/stories/0401_0111.html>.

67 Fielder, p. 237.

68 "Colorado Legends: Haunted St Elmo" n.d. Web 4 January 2013 <http://www.legendsofamerica.com/co-stelmo.html>.

69 John L. Sorenson and Carl L. Johannessen, *World Trade and Biological Exchanges Before 1492,* New York: iUniverse, 2004, 2009, p. 41.

70 "Huerfano River," Travel Colorado n.d. Web 14 November 2012 <http://www.travel.colorado.com/activities/summer/colorado/huerfano-river>.

71 "Species Indications" n.d. Web 14 November 2012 <http://www.wildlife.state.co.us/Fishing/SpeciesID/Pages/FishID.aspx>.

72 "Yellowfin Cutthroat Trout/Rocky Mountain Wild" n.d. Web 4 January 2013 <http://www.rockymountainwild.org/species/fish/yellowfin-cutthroat-trout>.

73 "The San Luis Valley Community Wetlands Strategy" September 2000 Web 19 December 2012 <http://www.wildlife.state.co.us/SiteCollectionDocuments/DOW/LandWater/WetlandsPrograms/stratplan-SLV9-00.pdf>.

74 Mark R. Guthrie, Powys Gadd, Renee Johnson, Joseph J. Lischka, *Colorado Mountains Prehistoric Context,* Denver: Colorado Historical Society, 1984, p.56.

75 "Road Trip: San Luis Valley, Colorado" n.d. Web 29 December 2012 <http://www.travel.nationalgeographic.com/travel/road-trips/san-luis-valley-colorado-road-trip/>.

76 "Scenic Drives USA: Los Caminos Antiguos Back Country Byway" n.d. Web 29 December 2012 <http://www.scenicdrivesusa.com/node/67>.

77 James E. Snead, Clark L. Erickson, and J. Andrew Darling, *Landscapes of Movement: Trails, Paths, and Roads in Anthropological Perspective,* Philadelphia: University of Pennsylvania Museum of Archaeology and Anthropology, 2006, p.21.

78 "Alamosa Community Guide" n.d. Web 14 November 2012 <http://www.cityofalamosa.org>.

79 *Visitor Guide: Great Sand Dunes National Park,* National Park Service, U.S. Department of the Interior.

80 *Great Sand Dunes: Great Sand Dunes National Park and Preserve Colorado,* National Park Service, US Department of the Interior.

81 Virginia T. McLemore and Gretchen Hoffman "Mineral Deposits in Rio Arriba County, New Mexico," *New Mexico Geological Society, 56 Field Conference Guidebook, Geology of the Chama Basin,* 2005, pp 445-456.

82 "Acequias and their Iberian Origins," New Mexico Office of the State Historian n.d. Web. 28 October 2012 <http://www.newmexicohistory.org/filedetails.php?fileID=22126>.

83 "Pueblo of Acoma: Big Game Trophy Hunts" n.d. Web 23 October 2012 <http://www.acomagameandfish.com>.

84 "Hakka" n.d. Web 25 October 2012 <http://www.encyclopedia.com/topic/Hakka.aspx>.

85 Charlotte Harris Rees, ed., *The Asiatic Fathers of America: Chinese Discovery and Colonization of Ancient America,* Lynchburg, VA: Warwick House, 2006, pp. 23, 98.

86 Anatole Andro, *The 1421 Heresy,* Bloomington, IN: Authorhouse, 2005, pp. 264-265.

87 Rees, *Secret Maps of the Ancient World,* p. 118.

88 Mertz, *Pale Ink,* pp. 26-36.

89 Mertz, *Pale Ink,* p. 39.

90 Franklin Folsom and Mary Elting Folsom, *Ancient Treasures of the Southwest,* Albuquerque: University of New Mexico Press, 1994, p. 85.

91 Vining, p. 219.

92 "Fort Union National Monument" n.d. Web 7 January 2013 <http://www.www.nps.gov/nr/travel/amsw/sw48.htm>.

93 *Historic Express St. James Hotel Cimarron, New Mexico,* Brochure.

94 Snead, pp. 122-125.

95 Malcolm Ebright, *The Manzano Mountain State Park: History of Title and History of the Manzano Land Grant,* Commission for Public Records pursuant to Contract #09-36099-00870, 6/15/2009. p. 6-7.

96 "Cibola" n.d. Web 6 November 2012 <http://www.merriam-webster.com/dictionary/cibola>.

97 "Minerals from New Mexico" n.d. Web 6 November, 2012 < http://www.johnbetts-fineminerals.com/jhbnyc/mineralmuseum/gallery2.php?init=&loc=New+Mexico>.

98 Travel the Historic Turquoise Trail National Scenic Byway: the Perfect Day Trip, brochure. <http://www.turquoisetrail.org>.

99 "Tree of Heaven" 7 July 2009 Web 24 October 2012 <http://www.nps.gov/plants/alien/fact/aial1.htm>.

100 Ebright, p. 10.

101 Robert C. Sivinski, "Checklist of Vascular Plants in the Sandia and Manzano Mountains of Central New Mexico," *Occasional Papers of the Museum of Southwestern Biology,* No. 10, 12 February 2007, pp. 1-67.

102 "Traditional Chinese Medicine: An Introduction" n.d. Web 29 January 2013 <http://www.nccam.nih.gov/health/whatiscam/chinesemed.htm>.

103 Jianping Zhang, Houyuan Lu, Naiqin Wu, Xiaoyan Yang, Xianmin Diao, "Phytolith Analysis for Differentiating between Foxtail Millet (Setaria italica) and Green Foxtail (Setaria viridis)" 31 January 2011 Web 19 January 2013 <http://www.plosone.org/article.info%3Adoi%2F10.1371%2Fjournal.pone.0019726>.

104 Vining, pp. 661-664.

105 E. N. Anderson, *Everyone Eats: Understanding Food and Culture,* New York: NYU Press, 2005, p. 86.

106 Where plants had multiple uses I listed them in the following priority. First - Traditional Chinese Medicines, Second - a food or beverage, Third – grass or animal feed. Each plant was only counted in one category. Therefore, there were a few additional types of grass besides the nine mentioned in this chapter. Those other grasses had other uses besides animal feed.

Endnotes

107 Arthur H. Harris, "Plio-Pleistocene Vertebrate Fossils of the El Paso Area," El Paso, TX: Laboratory for Environmental Biology, Centennial Museum, University of Texas at El Paso, No. 6, 3 April 2000.

108 Rees, *Secret Maps of the Ancient World,* p. 82.

109 Jie Bao, "The history of horse using in Xia and Shang Dynasties," Horse, Indo-Europeans Spread and the Rising of Zhou Dynasty 12 December 2002 Web 23 January 2013 <http://www.cs.iastate.edu/~baojie/history/chinese/2002-12-02_horse.en.htm>.

110 Vining, p. 667.

111 Vining, p. 286.

112 "Welcome to the City of Albuquerque: Chinese Americans," n.d. Web 4 November 2012 <http://www.cabq.gov/humanrights/public-information-and-education/diversity-booklets/asian-and-pacific-island-heritage-in-new-mexico/chinese-americans>.

113 David E. Stuart and Rory P. Gauthier, *Prehistoric New Mexico: Background for Survey,* Albuquerque: University of New Mexico Press, 1988, p. 128.

114 Roger Spencer, Rob Cross, Peter Lumley, *Plant Names: A Guide to Botanical Nomenclature,* Australia: CSIRO Publishing, 2007, p. 47.

115 Charlie Custer, "Chinese Invented the Totem Pole" 14 December 2010 Web. 6 November 2012 <www.theworldofChinese.com/2010/12/china-invented-the-totem-pole/>.

116 *Boca Negra Canyon Trail Guide: Petroglyph National Monument,* Publication of National Park Service and City of Albuquerque.

117 John A. Ruskamp, Jr., *Asiatic Echoes: The Identification of Chinese Pictograms in North American Rock Writing,* Create Space Publishing, 2011, 2013.

118 "Chinese/Chinese character meaning" n.d. Web 5 January 2013 <http://www.en.allexperts.com/q/Chinese-2782/2012/7/chinese-character-meaning.htm>.

119 Lynne D. Escue, "Chaco Culture National Historical Park" n.d. Web 8 January 2013 <http://www.firstpeople.us/articles/Chaco-Culture/The-Evidence-Chaco-Society-Technology-And-Trade.html>.

120 *Galisteo Basin Archaeological Sites Protection Act: General Management Plan,* US Department of the Interior, Bureau of Land Management, Taos, NM Field Office, July 2012.

121 John A. Ruskamp, Jr., *Asiatic Echoes: The Identification of Chinese Pictograms in North American Rock Writing: Addendum 2012,* Create Space Publishing, p. 12.

122 *Petroglyph National Monument,* Tucson: Western National Park Association, 1993, 2005, p.13.

123 Stuart, p. 76.

124 Stuart, p. 319.

125 W. James Judge, *Paleoindian Occupation: of the Central Rio Grande Valley in New Mexico,* Albuquerque: University of New Mexico Press, 1977, p. 48.

126 "The Origins of Taoism" 11 December 2009 Web 10 December 2012 <http://www.bbc.co.uk/religion/religions/taoism/history/history.shtml>.

127 "History of Taoism" n.d. Web 10 December 2012 < http://www.history.cultural-china.com/en/1661History5044.html>.

128 "House Architecture" n.d. Web 10 December 2012 <http://www.depts.washington.edu/chinaclv/3intrhme.htm>.

129 "High Rolls Cave," New Mexico Office of Archaeological Studies n.d. Web 25 November 2012 <http://www.nmarchaeology.org/high-rolls-cave.html>.

130 Thomas R. Rocek and John D. Speth, *The Henderson Site Burials: Glimpses of a Late Prehistoric Population in the Pecos Valley,* Ann Arbor: University of Michigan, 1986.

131 Temple, pp. 191-195 and 280-281.

132 Miriam Lowrance, "Rock Art of Jeff Davis County Part I and II," *The Artifact,* Vol. 25, No. 2, p. 99.

133 "Sierra Blanca" n.d. Web 17 December 2012 <http://www.mescaleroapache.com/area/sierra_blanca.htm>.

134 Martha L. Henderson, "Sacred Sites Sustaining Tribal Economies: the Mescalero Apache" 25 November 2007 Web 17 December 2012 <http://www.nativecases.evergreen.edu/.../SacredSites-Henderson_Nov_25_2007.doc>.

135 "Ski Apache" n.d. Web 17 December 2012 <http://www.onthesnow.com/new-mexico/ski-apache/ski-resort.html>.

136 Tanya Dewey and Julia Smith, "Canis Lupus gray wolf" n.d. Web 7 November 2012 <http://www.animaldiversity.ummz.umich.edu/site/accounts/information/Canis_lupus.html>.

137 Robert H. Weber, "Petroglyphs of the Sierra Blanca," *New Mexico Geological Society Fifteenth Field Conference*, Socorro, New Mexico, 1964, p. 177.

138 Simon G. Southerton, *Losing a Lost Tribe,* Salt Lake City: Signature Books, 2004, pp. 96-97.

139 William C. Martin, *Some Aspect of the Natural History of the Capitan and Jicarilla Mountains, and Sierra Blanca Region of New Mexico*, New Mexico Geological Society, Guidebook 15, Albuquerque: University of New Mexico, 1964, pp. 171-176.

140 "Scenic Trips to the Geologic Past # 3: Roswell-Ruidoso-Valley of Fires, including trips to Lincoln, Tularosa, and Bottomless Lakes State Park" n.d. Web 17 December 2012 <http://www.geoinfo.nmt.edu/publications/scenictrips/3/>.

Endnotes

141 Ibid.

142 Rex Johnson, Jr., and Ron Smoryoski, *Fly Fishing in Southern New Mexico,* Albuquerque: University of New Mexico Press, 1998, p. 149.

143 "Salmo trutta," p. 3.

144 "Fishing: Visitor Information" n.d. Web 8 November 2012 <www.ruidoso.net/visitors/outdoors/fishing.html>.

145 Stuart, pp. 232 – 234.

146 Weber, p. 177.

147 "Mammals: Taxonomy and Natural History Labs, Mammal Skins, part A, Biol. 452, Vertebrate Biology" 2012 Web 7 November 2012 <http://www.courses.washington.edu.../labs/452mammal-skins-summer-2012b.pdf.>.

148 Julio L. Betancourt, Kate Aasen Rylander, Cristina Penalba, Janet L. McVickar, "Late Quaternary vegetation history of Rough Canyon, south-central New Mexico, USA," *Palaeogeography, Palaeoclimatology, Palaeoecology* 165 (2001), p. 74.

149 *Guadalupe Mountains,* National Park Service, U.S. Department of the Interior.

150 Philip Burke King, *Geology of the Southern Guadalupe Mountains, Texas,* U.S. Geological Survey, 1948, pp 148-151.

151 "This Bites: Venomous Texas Snakes" n.d. Web 20 November 2012 <https://www.dshs.state.tx.us/idcu/health/zoonosis/animal/bites/information/venom/snake/>.

152 "Trans-Pecos Mountains and Basins," Vegetational Areas of Texas n. d. Web 20 November 2012 <http://www.uta.edu/biology/meik/classnotes/.../TexasVegetationLect/.pdf>.

153 "Mineral Resources and Mining," Texas State Historical Association n.d. Web 20 November 2012 <http://www.tshaonline.org/handbook/online/articles/gpm01>.

154 J. Frank Dobie, "Secret of the Guadalupes," *Coronado's Children,* 1930, pp. 256 – 267, <http://www.odessahistory.com/dobiesst.htm>.

155 Ibid.

156 "Treasure with Bill Burrud 1958 – Ben Sublett's Gold Mine" 19 May 2008 Web 21 November 2012 <http://www.youtube.com/watch?v=giAkVKTZ_i0>.

157 Rees, *Secret Maps of the Ancient World,* p. 84.

158 "Rock Art: Trans-Pecos" n.d. Web 21 November 2012 <http://www.texasbeyondhistory.net/trans-p/artistic/index.htm>.

159 "Guadalupe Mountains," n.d. Web 20 November, 2012 <http://www.tshaonline.org/handbook/online/articles/rjg18>.

160 Ellis W. Shuler, "Collecting Fossil Elephants at Dallas, Texas," *Field & Laboratory,* Nov. 1934, Vol. III, No. 1, p. 24 (reprinted by permission from *Bulletin of the Texas Archeological and Paleontological Society,* September 1934, Vol. 6, pp. 75-79).

161 Rees, *Secret Maps of the Ancient World,* pp. 136-137.

162 Ruskamp, Addendum 2012, p. 34.

163 "Mammoth Rocks," n.d. Web 19 November 2012 <http://www.parks.ca.gov/?page_id=23566>.

164 A. T. Jackson, *Picture Writing of the Texas Indians,* Anthropological Papers, Vol. II, Austin: The University of Texas, 1938, pp. 48-49.

165 "Lobo Valley Petroglyph Site," Texas State Historical Association n.d. Web 7 December 2012 <http://www.tshaonline.org/handbook/online/articles/bbl10>.

166 Frank H. Chalfant, "Early Chinese Writing," *Memoirs of the Carnegie Museum*, Pittsburgh: Carnegie Institute, 1906. (This is available online or as a reprint.)

167 "Davis Mountains Preserve: A Visitor's Guide," The Nature Conservancy 2012 Web 18 December 2012 <http://www.fortdavis.com/2012TNCGuide.pdf>.

168 "Sus Scrofa (Feral Pig)" Smithsonian Marine Station at Fort Pierce n.d. Web 29 November 2012 <http://www.sms.si.edu/irlspec/sus_scofa.htm>.

169 Sheldon L. Glover, *Origin and Occurrence of Gem Stones in Washington,* Olympia, WA: Department of Conservation and Development, State of Washington, Division of Mines and Geology, Report of Investigations No. 16, 1949, pp. 7-8.

170 "Archeologists Investigate Wolf Den Cave," Center for Big Bend Studies: Trans-Pecos Archeological Program n.d. Web 9 December 2012 <http://www.sulross.edu/cbbs/tap-wolfden.php>.

171 Miriam Lowrance, "Rock Art of Jeff Davis County Part I and II," *The Artifact,* Vol. 25, No. 2, p. 127.

172 Ibid.

173 "Cueva Pilote" n.d. Web 5 December 2012 <http://www,texasbeyondhistory.net/pilote/html>.

174 Bagrow, p. 197.

175 "Trans Pecos Mountains and Basins: Artistic Expression" n.d. Web 5 December 2012 <http://www.texasbeyondhistory.net/trans-p/artistic/index.html>.

176 Copies of these journals can be ordered through the website of El Paso Archaeological Society at www.epas.com

177 "Travelers Discover Heritage, Natural Wonders in Texas Mountain Trail Region" Travel Texas. Web <http://www.thc.state.tx.us/medallionmag/medalliontravelPDFS/mt_trl_rgn_10.pdf>.

178 Jackson, p. 72.

179 John A. Hedrick, "Van Horn Quarries" 1989 Web 15 November 2012 <http://www.texasbeyondhistory.net/trans-p/nature/images/vanhorn-quarries.html>.

180 "Wild Cane," The Portal to Texas History n.d. Web 15 November 2012 <http://www.texashistory.unt.edu/ark:/67531/metapth88028/>.

Endnotes

181 Miriam A. Lowrance, "Rock Art of Presidio County," *The Artifact,* Vol. 26, No. 3, El Paso: El Paso Archaeological Society, 1988, p. 3.

182 Ibid.

183 Rees, *Secret Maps of the Ancient World,* p. 52.

184 Rees, *Secret Maps of the Ancient World,* pp. 44-45.

185 "Plant Fact Sheet: Texas Kidneywood (Eysenhardtia texana)" n.d. Web 14 November 2012 <http://www.plant-materials.nrcs.usda.gov/pubs/stpmcfsplantguide.pdf>.

186 Elbert A. King, Jr. *Texas Gemstones*, Report of Investigations – No. 42, Bureau of Economic Geology, Austin: The University of Texas at Austin, 1961, p. 27.

187 "Presidio, TX," U.S. Climate Data n.d. Web 17 November 2012 <http://www.usclimatedata.com/climate.php?location=USTX1094>.

188 "Presidio, TX," Texas State Historical Association, n.d. Web 17 November 2012 <http://www.tshaonline.org/handbook/online/articles/hjp13>.

189 Stuart, p. 184.

190 Ruth Shady Solis, Jonathan Haas, Winifred Creamer, "Dating Caral, a Preceramic Site in the Supe Valley on the Central Coast of Peru," *Science,* Vol. 292, 27 April 2001, pp 723-726.

191 Sorenson and Johannessen, p. 13.

192 "La Junta de los Rios: Villagers of the Chihuahuan Desert Rivers" n.d. Web 17 November 2012 <http://www.texasbeyondhistory.net/junta/index.html>.

193 Ibid.

194 Lowrance, *The Artifact,* Vol. 26, No. 3, p. 1.

195 "La Junta de los Rios: Chronology: Archeological Time" n.d. Web 17 November 2012 <http://www.texasbeyondhistory.net/junta/chronology.html>.

196 "Ceremonial Cave: Artifact Gallery," n.d. Web 5 December 2012 <www.texasbeyondhistory.net/ceremonial/gallery.html.>.

197 Lowrance, *The Artifact,* Vol. 26, No. 3, p. 27.

198 Kwang-Chih Chang, *Shang Civilization,* New Haven and London: Yale University Press, 1980, pp 332-335.

199 Christopher L.C.E. Witcombe, "Stonehenge," Art History Resources n.d. Web 23 November 2012 <http://www.arthistoryresources.net/stonehenge/archaeoastronomy.html>.

200 Ibid.

201 Gari Ledyard, "Cartography in Korea, Japan, and Vietnam," *History of Cartography* (Vol. 2, Bk 2), *Cartography in the Traditional East and Southeast Asian Societies,* Chicago: The University of Chicago Press, 1995, pp. 260-261.

202 Covey, 2005, p. 38.

203 Rees, *Secret Maps of the Ancient World*, pp. 135-138.

204 Miriam Lowrance, "Rock Art of Jeff Davis County," *The Artifact,* Vol. 25, No. 2, El Paso: El, p. 127.

205 Charles O. Hucker, *China to 1850: A Short History,* Stanford: Stanford University Press, 1975, 1976, 1978.

206 Pan Ku, *The History of the Former Han Dynasty,* Vol. III, tr. by Homer H. Dubs, Baltimore: Waverly Press, 1955, p. 214-215.

207 Pan Ku, pp. 511-515.

208 Lisa Flam, "100-Ounce Gold Nugget Could Fetch $400,000" 5 January 2011 Web 13 December 2012 <http://www.aolnews.com/2011/01/05/100-ounce-gold-nugget-found-in-california-could-fetch-400-000/>.

Bibliography

"Acequias and their Iberian Origins." New Mexico Office of the State Historian n.d. Web 28 October 2012 <http://www.newmexicohistory.org/filedetails.php?fileID=22126>.

"Alamosa Community Guide" n.d. Web 14 November 2012 <http://www.cityofalamosa.org>.

Albuquerque: The Official Visitors Guide and Vacation Planner. Albuquerque: 2012.

"An Amazing Past" n.d. Web 2 January 2012 < http://www.leadville.org/an-amazing-past.html>.

"Ancient Observatories Timeless Knowledge: Bighorn Medicine Wheel" n.d. Web 18 October 2012 <http://www.solar-center.stanford.edu/AO/bighorn.html>.

Anderson, E. N. *Everyone Eats: Understanding Food and Culture.* New York: NYU Press, 2005.

Andro, Anatole. *The 1421 Heresy.* Bloomington, IN: Authorhouse, 2005.

"Archeologists Investigate Wolf Den Cave." Center for Big Bend Studies: Trans-Pecos Archeological Program n.d. Web 9 December 2012 <http://www.sulross.edu/cbbs/tap-wolfden.php>.

Bagrow, Leo. *History of Cartography.* revised and enlarged by R. A. Skelton, Cambridge: Harvard University Press, 1966.

Bao, Jia, "The history of horse using in Xia and Shang Dynasties." *Horse, Indo-Europeans Spread and the Rising of Zhou Dynasty.* 12 December 2002 Web 23 January 2013 <http://www.cs.iastate.edu/~baojie/history/chinese/2002-12-02_horse.en.htm>.

Barkley, R.A. "The Kuroshio Current" 1973 Web 10 December 2012 <http://www.swfsc.noaa.gov/publications/CR/1973/7302.PDF>.

Bartlett, I.S., ed. *History of Wyoming,* Vol. I. Chicago: The S. J. Clarke Publishing Company, 1918.

Bassan, Nasir El. *Handbook of Bioenergy Crops: A Complete Reference to Species Development and Applications.* Oxford, UK: Routledge, 2010.

Betancourt, Julio L, Kate Aasen Rylander, Cristina Penalba, Janet L. McVickar. "Late Quaternary vegetation history of Rough Canyon, south-central New Mexico, USA." *Palaeogeography, Palaeoclimatology, Palaeoecology* 165 (2001).

Boca Negra Canyon Trail Guide, Petroglyph National Monument. Publication of National Parks Service and City of Albuquerque.

"Boulder Monuments" n.d. Web 19 October 2012 <http://www.esask.uregina.ca/tmc_cms/modules/customcode/includes/print_entry.cfm?entryid=7344226D-1560-95>.

"Buffalo Soldiers at Fort Davis." National Park Service, US Department of the Interior n.d. Web 7 December 2012 <http://www.nps.gov/foda/forteachers/upload/buffalosoldiers.pdf>.

Cassells, E. Steve. *The Archaeology of Colorado.* Boulder, CO: Johnson Books, 1997.

"Ceremonial Cave: Artifact Gallery" n.d. Web 5 December 2012 <www.texasbeyondhistory.net/ceremonial/gallery.html.>.

Chalfant, Frank H. "Early Chinese Writing," *Memoirs of the Carnegie Museum.* Pittsburgh: Carnegie Institute, 1906.

Chang, Kwang-Chih. *The Archaeology of Ancient China.* New Haven, CT: Yale University Press, 1972.

___. *Early Chinese Civilization: Anthropological Perspectives.* Cambridge, MA: Harvard University Press, 1976.

___. *Shang Civilization.* New Haven and London: Yale University Press, 1980.

___. ed. *Studies of Shang Archaeology: Selected Papers from the International Conference on Shang Civilization.* New Haven, CT: Yale University Press, 1986.

"Chinese/Chinese character meaning" n.d. Web 5 January 2013 <http://www.en.allexperts.com/q/Chinese-2782/2012/7/chinese-character-meaning.htm>.

"Cibola" n.d. Web 6 November 2012 <http://www.merriam-webster.com/dictionary/cibola>.

Bibliography

"Collared Peccary." Desert USA n.d. Web 29 November 2012 <http://www.desertusa.com/magnov97/nov-pap/du_collpecc.html>.

"Collared Peccary." The Mammals of Texas n.d. Web 28 November 2012 <http://www.nsrl.ttu.edu/tmot1/tayataja.htm>.

"Colorado Legends: Haunted St. Elmo" n.d. Web 4 January 2013 <http://www.legendsofamerica.com/co-stelmo.html>.

"Colorado Legends: Leadville-Cloud City" n.d. Web 2 January 2013 <http://www.legendsofamerica.com/co-leadville.html>.

"Continental Divide National Scenic Trail." National Park Service n.d. Web. 11 October 2012 <http://www.nps.gov/romo/planyourvisit/divide.htm>.

"Continental Divide Peaks – Colorado" 6 August 2012 Web. 11 October 2012 <http://www.summitpost.org/continental-divide-peaks-colorado/172039>.

Covey, Cyclone. *A Critical Reprise of 'Aboriginal' American History.* Winston Salem, NC: Wake Forest University, 2000 – 2005.

"Crystal Mountain Pegmatite District (Storm Mountain District), Larimer Co., Colorado, USA Mineral List" n.d. Web. 10 September 2012 < http://www.mindat.org/loc-8251.html>.

"Cueva Pilote" n.d. Web 5 December 2012 <http://www.texasbeyondhistory.net/pilote/html>.

Custer, Charlie. "Chinese Invented the Totem Pole" 14 December 2010, Web. 6 November 2012 <http:www.theworldofChinese.com/2010/12/china-invented-the-totem-pole/>.

"Davis Mountains Preserve: A Visitor's Guide." The Nature Conservancy 2012 Web 18 December 2012 <http://www.fortdavis.com/2012TNCGuide.pdf>.

Dematte, Paola. "The Rock Art of Inner Mongolia & Ningxia." n.d. Web 12 May 2013 <http://www.bradshawfoundation.com/china/ningxia/index.php>.

Deng, Gang. *Chinese Maritime Activities and Socioeconomic Development, c. 2100 B.C. – 1900 A.D.* London: Greenwood Press, 1997.

De Vaca, Cabeza. *Adventures in the Unknown Interior of America.* tr. by Cyclone Covey, Albuquerque: University of New Mexico Press, 1997.

"The Devil's Gate" n.d. Web. 8 October 2012 <http://www.wyoshpo.state.wy.us/trailsdemo/devilsgate.htm>.

"Devil's Gate – California National Historic Trail." National Park Service n.d. Web 8 October 2012 <http://www.nps.gov/cali/planyourvisit/site6.htm>.

Dewey, Tanya and Julia Smith. "Canis Lupus gray wolf." Animal Diversity n.d. Web 7 November 2012 <http://www.animaldiversity.ummz.umich.edu/site/accounts/information/Canis_lupus.html>.

Dobie, J. Frank. "Secret of the Guadalupes." *Coronado's Children,* 1930 Web 20 November 2012 <http://www.odessahistory.com/dobiesst.htm>.

"Dream Stream (South Platte) – Half Day" n.d. Web 22 October 2012 <http://www.arkanglers.com/dream-stream-south-platte-half-day>.

Duguid, James and Gabriel Bedish. *An Analysis of the Spanish Diggings Region of Wyoming During Paleolithic Inhabitation.* WyAr 11(1) Part 2, Wyoming Archaeological Society, 1968.

Ebbesmeyer, Curtis & Eric Scigliano. *Flotsametrics and the Floating World: How One Man's Obsession with Runaway Sneakers and Rubber Ducks Revolutionized Ocean Science.* New York: Smithsonian Books, 2009.

Ebright, Malcolm. *The Manzano Mountain State Park: History of Title and History of the Manzano Land Grant.* Commission for Public Records pursuant to Contract #09-36099-00870, 6/15/2009.

Eddy, John A. "Astronomical Alignment of the Big Horn Medicine Wheel." *Science,* Vol. 184, No. 4141, 7 June 1974.

Escue, Lynne D. "Chaco Culture National Historical Park" n.d. Web 8 January 2013 <http://www.firstpeople.us/articles/Chaco-Culture/The-Evidence-Chaco-Society-Technology-And-Trade.html>.

Estes Park, Colorado: Official Visitor Guide. Greensboro, NC: Pace Communications, 2012.

Fielder, John. *John Fielder's Best of Colorado.* Englewood, CO: Westcliffe Publishers, 2004.

Bibliography

"Fishing:Visitor Information" n.d. Web 8 November 2012 <www.ruidoso.net/visitors/outdoors/fishing.html>.

FitzGerald, Michael. "Portals to Other Realities." *Wall Street Journal* 18 September 2010 Web 8 June 2013 <http://www.online.wsj.com/artile/SB10001424052748704644404575482342261278092.html>.

Flam, Lisa. "100-Ounce Gold Nugget Could Fetch $400,000" 5 January 2011 Web 13 December 2012 <http://www.aolnews.com/2011/01/05/100-ounce-gold-nugget-found-in-california-could-fetch-400-000/>.

Fogelberg, Ben. *Walking Into Colorado's Past: 50 Front Range History Hikes.* Boulder, CO: Westcliff Publishers Inc., 2006.

Folsom, Franklin. *Indian Uprising on the Rio Grande: The Pueblo Revolt of 1680.* Albuquerque: University of New Mexico Press, 1973.

Folsom, Franklin and Mary Elting Folsom. *Ancient Treasures of the Southwest.* Albuquerque: University of New Mexico Press, 1994.

"Fort Davis, Texas" n.d. Web 7 December 2012 <http://www.texasescapes.com/WestTexasTowns/FtDavisTx/FortDavisTexas.htm>.

"Fort Davis, Texas: The History." Chamber of Commerce n.d. Web 7 December 2012 <http://www.fortdavis.com/history.html>.

"Fort Union National Monument" n.d. Web 7 January 2013 <http://www.www.nps.gov/nr/travel/amsw/sw48.htm>.

Frase, Barbara A. and Robert S. Hoffmann. "Marmota Flaviventris." *Mammalian Species* (The American Society of Mammalogists) No. 135, 15 April 1980.

Galisteo Basin Archaeological Sites Protection Act: General Management Plan. US Department of the Interior, Bureau of Land Management, Taos, NM Field Office, July 2012.

Gardner, Mark L. *Santa Fe Trail: National Historic Trail.* Western National Parks Association, 1993, 2008.

Glover, Sheldon L. *Origin and Occurrence of Gem Stones in Washington.* Report of Investigations No. 16, Olympia, WA: Department of Conservation and Development State of Washington, Division of Mines and Geology, 1949.

"Grays and Torreys Trail" n.d. Web 5 September 2012 <http://www.sangres.com/colorado/national-forests/arapaho/trails/graysandtorreys-54htm>.

"Grays Peak and Torreys Peak" n.d. Web 30 July 2013 <http://www.protrails.com/trail/summit-county-eagle-county-clear-creek-county-grays-peak-and-torreys-peak>.

"Grays Peak – Torreys Peak" n.d. Web 2 January 2013 <http://www.cloudhiking.com/mountains/rockies/grays-torreys.php>.

Great Sand Dunes: Great Sand Dunes National Park and Preserve Colorado. National Park Service, US Department of the Interior.

Great Sand Dunes: What's Growing? National Park Service, US Department of the Interior.

"Guadalupe Mountains" n.d. Web 20 November 2012 <http://www.tshaonline.org/handbook/online/articles/rjg18>.

"Guadalupe Mountains National Park Information Page" n.d. Web 3 December 2012 <http://www.guadalupe.mountains.national-park.com/info.htm>.

Guadalupe Mountains. National Park Service, US Department of the Interior.

Guthrie, Mark R., Powys Gadd, Renee Johnson, Joseph J. Lischka. *Colorado Mountains Prehistoric Context*. Denver: Colorado Historical Society, 1984.

"Hakka" n.d. Web. 25 October 2012 <http://www.encyclopedia.com/topic/Hakka.aspx>.

"The Hakka People" n.d. Web 25 October 2012 <http://www.edu.ocac.gov.tw/lan/hakka/englisha/a.htm>.

Harris, Arthur H. "Plio-Pleistocene Vertebrate Fossils of the El Paso Area." El Paso, TX: Laboratory for Environmental Biology, Centennial Museum, University of Texas at El Paso, No. 6, 3 April 2000.

Harris, Hendon M. *The Asiatic Fathers of America* (Two Books in One Volume): 1. *The Chinese Discovery and Colonization of Ancient America* 2. *The Asiatic Kingdoms of America*. Taipei: Wen Ho Printing Company, 1973.

Hausel, W. Dan. *Guide to the Geology, Mining Districts and Ghost Towns of Medicine Bow and Snowy Ridge Scenic Byway*. Public Information Circular No. 32, Laramie, WY: The Geological Survey of Wyoming, 1993.

Bibliography

___. *Mining History and Geology of Some of Wyoming's Metal and Gemstone Districts and Deposits.* Reprint No. 56, Laramie, WY: The Geological Survey of Wyoming, 1994.

Hedrick, John A. "Van Horn Quarries" n.d. Web 15 November 2012 <http://www.texasbeyondhistory.net/trans-p/nature/images/vanhorn-quarries.html>.

Henderson, Martha L. "Sacred Sites Sustaining Tribal Economies: the Mescalero Apache" 25 November 2007 Web 17 December 2012 <http://www.nativecases.evergreen.edu/.../SacredSites-Henderson_Nov_25_2007.doc>.

"High Rolls Cave." New Mexico Office of Archaeological Studies n.d. Web 25 November 2012 <http://www.nmarchaeology.org/high-rolls-cave.html>.

"The Highest Mountain Peaks in Colorado" n.d. Web 18 October 2012 <http://www.sangres.com/mountains/index1.htm>.

Hildebrandt, Laura. *Unbroken: A World War II Story of Survival, Resilience, and Redemption.* New York: Random House, 2010.

Historic Express St. James Hotel Cimarron, New Mexico. Brochure.

"History of Taoism" n.d. Web 10 December 2012 <http://www.history.cultural-china.com/en/1661History5044.html>.

Hobson, John M. *The Eastern Origins of Western Civilisation.* Cambridge: Cambridge University Press, 2004.

Holleran, Michael. *Historic Context for Irrigation and Water Supply Ditches and Canals in Colorado.* Denver: University of Colorado at Denver, June 2005.

"House Architecture" n.d. Web 10 December 2012 <http://www.depts.washington.edu/chinaclv/3intrhme.htm>.

Hucker, Charles O. *China to 1850: A Short History,* Stanford: Stanford University Press, 1975, 1976, 1978.

"Huerfano River." Travel Colorado n.d. Web 14 November 2012 <http://www.travelcolorado.com/activities/summer/colorado/huerfano-river>.

"Independence Rock." Oregon - California Trails Association n.d. Web 15 December 2012 <http://www.octa-trails.org/learn/virtual_tour/virtual_tour/independence_rock/index.php>.

Jackson, A. T. *Picture Writing of Texas Indians.* Austin: University of Texas Press, 1938.

Johnson, Jr., Rex, and Ron Smoryoski. *Fly Fishing in Southern New Mexico.* Albuquerque: University of New Mexico Press, 1998.

Judge, W. James. *Paleoindian Occupation: of the Central Rio Grande Valley in New Mexico.* Albuquerque: University of New Mexico Press, 1977.

Kern, Stephen J. "Bats in Chinese Art." *Bats Magazine,* Vol. 6, No. 4 Winter 1988 <http://www.batcon.org/index.php/media-and-info/bats-archives.html?task=viewArticle&magArticleID=369>.

Kever, Jeannie. "W. Texas becomes more lonely as population drops." *Houston Chronicle* 12 April 2011 web 20 November 2012 <http://www.chron.com/news/houston-texas/...W-Texas-becomes-more-lonely-as-population-drops-1692706.php>.

King, Jr., Elbert A. *Texas Gemstones.* Report of Investigations – No. 42, Austin: Bureau of Economic Geology, Austin: The University of Texas at Austin, 1961.

King, Philip Burke. *Geology of the Southern Guadalupe Mountains, Texas.* US Geological Survey, 1948.

Koschmann, A.H. and M. H. Bergendahl. *Principal Gold-Producing Districts of the United States.* Geological Survey Professional Paper 610, Washington, DC: United States Government Printing Office, 1968.

"La Junta de los Rios: Chronology: Archeological Time" n.d. Web 17 November 2012 <http://www.texasbeyondhistory.net/junta/chronology.html>.

"La Junta de los Rios: Villagers of the Chihuahuan Desert Rivers" n.d. Web 17 November 2012 <http://www.texasbeyondhistory.net/junta/index.html.>.

"Leadville Attractions" n.d. Web 2 January 2013 <http://www.visitleadvilleco.com/attractions>.

"Leadville History: 1878-1893" n.d. Web 2 January 2013 <http://www.visitleadvilleco.com/history>.

Ledyard, Gari. "Cartography in Korea, Japan, and Vietnam." *The History of Cartography* Vol. 2, Bk. 2, *Cartography in the Traditional East and Southeast Asian Societies,* Chicago: The University of Chicago Press, 1995.

Bibliography

"Lobo Valley Petroglyph Site." Texas State Historical Association n.d. Web 7 December 2012 <http://www.tshaonline.org/handbook/online/articles/bbl10>.

"The Louisiana Purchase 'Opens' the West: Other Explorers Follow Lewis & Clark: Stephen H. Long" n.d. Web 22 October 2012 <http://www.nebraskastudies.org/0400/stories/0401_0111.html>.

Lowrance, Miriam A. "Rock Art of Jeff Davis County Part I and II." *The Artifact*, Vol. 25, No. 2, El Paso: El Paso Archaeological Society, Inc., 1987.

___. "Rock Art of Jeff Davis County Part III and IV." *The Artifact*, Vol. 25, No. 3, El Paso: El Paso Archaeological Society, Inc., 1987.

___. "Rock Art of Presidio County Part 1 and 2." *The Artifact*, Vol. 26, No. 3, El Paso: El Paso Archaeological Society, Inc., 1988.

___. "Rock Art of Presidio County Part 3." *The Artifact*, Vol. 26, No. 4, El Paso: El Paso Archaeological Society, Inc., 1988.

"Major Issues and Findings – Welcome to the Rio Grande Valley." US Geological Survey n.d. Web 30 October 2012 <http://www.pubs.usgs.gov/circ/circ1162/nawqa91.4.html>.

"Mammals: Taxonomy and Natural History Labs, Mammal Skins, Part A, Biol. 452, Vertebrate Biology" 2012 Web 7 November 2012 <http://www.courses.washington.edu.../labs/452mammal-skins-summer-2012b.pdf.>.

"Mammoth Rocks" n.d. Web 19 November 2012 <http://www.parks.ca.gov/?page_id=23566>.

Martin, William C. *Some Aspect of the Natural History of the Capitan and Jicarilla Mountains, and Sierra Blanca Region of New Mexico.* New Mexico Geological Society, Guidebook 15, Albuquerque: University of New Mexico, 1964.

McCoy, Michael. *Off the Beaten Path Wyoming: A Guide to Unique Places.* Guilford, CT: Globe Pequot Press, 2010.

"The McKean Complex." University of Manitoba n.d. Web 4 October 2012 <http://www.umanitoba.ca/faculties/arts/anthropology/manarchnet/chronology/archaic/mckean.html>.

McKinney, Lee & Tag McKinney. *Colorado Gems & Minerals.* Phoenix, AZ: Renaissance House Publishers, 1987.

McLemore, Virginia T. and Gretchen Hoffman. "Mineral Deposits in Rio Arriba County, New Mexico." *New Mexico Geological Society, 56th Field Conference Guidebook, Geology of the Chama Basin.* 2005.

Mertz, Henriette. *Gods from the Far East: How the Chinese Discovered America.* New York: Ballantine Books, 1972.

___. *Pale Ink.* Chicago, 1953.

"Mineral Resources and Mining." Texas State Historical Association n.d. Web 20 November 2012 <http://www.tshaonline.org/handbook/online/articles/gpm01>.

"Minerals from New Mexico" n.d. Web 6 November 2012 <http://www.johnbetts-fineminerals.com/jhbnyc/mineralmuseum/gallery2.php?init=&loc=New+Mexico>.

National Historic Trails: Auto Tour Route Interpretive Guide, Across Wyoming. Salt Lake City: National Park Service, 2007.

"National Register of Historic Places Inventory Nomination Form." Libby Lodge, Snowy Range Lodge, 30 September 1976 Web 18 November 2012 <http://www.pdfhost.focus.nps.gov/docs/NRHP/Text/76001947.pdf>.

Needham, Joseph. *Clerks and Craftsmen in China and the West.* Cambridge: University Press, 1970.

___. *Science and Civilisation in China.* Vol. 4 Physics and Physical Technology, Part 3 "Civil Engineering and Nautics." Cambridge: Cambridge University Press, 1971.

"New Mexico Gold Map." Gold Maps Online n.d. Web 23 October 2012 <http://www.goldmapsonline.com/new-mexico-gold-map.html>.

"New Mexico Mountain Lion Hunts, Dangerously Big Cats!" n.d. Web 17 September 2012 <http://www.sierrablancaoutfitters.com/new-mexico-mountain-lion-hunts/>.

"New Mexico Summits above 11,000 Feet" n.d. Web 23 October 2012 <http://www/americasroof.com/highest/nm.shtml>.

"Official Song of the State of Kansas" n.d. Web 9 October 2012 <http://www.50states.com/songs/kansas.htm#.UHR9ARVfB2A>.

"The Origins of Taoism" 11 December 2009 Web 10 December 2012 <http://www.bbc.co.uk/religon/religions/taoism/history/history.shtml>.

Pan Ku. *The History of the Former Han Dynasty*. Vol. III, tr. by Homer H. Dubs, Baltimore: Waverly Press, 1955.

Petroglyph National Monument. Tucson: Western National Parks Association, 1993, 2005.

"Plant Fact Sheet: Texas Kidneywood (Eysenhardtia texana)" n.d. Web 14 November 2012 <http://www.plant-materials.nrcs.usda.gov/pubs/stpmcfsplantguide.pdf.>.

"Presidio, TX." Texas State Historical Association n.d. Web 17 November 2012 <http://www.tshaonline.org/handbook/online/articles/hjp13>.

"Presidio, TX." US Climate Data n.d. Web 17 November 2012 <http://www.usclimatedata.com/climate.php?location=USTX1094>.

"Printable GPS Map for Continental Divide Trail in Wyoming" n.d. Web. 11 October 2012 <http://www.trailsource.com/continental-divide-trail/continental-divide-trail-map.asp?state=Wyoming>.

"Pronghorn." National Wildlife Federation n.d. Web 5 September 2012 <http://www.nwf.org/Wildlife/Wildlife-Library/Mammals/Pronghorn.aspx>.

"Pronghorn Antelope." Arizona Game & Fish Department n.d. Web 12 October 2012 <http://www.azgfd.gov/w_c/conservation/CGMP/CGMP-Pronghorn.pdf>.

"Pueblo of Acoma: Big Game Trophy Hunts" n.d. Web 23 October 2012 <http://www.acomagameandfish.com>.

"Rawah Wilderness Area" n.d. Web 14 November 2012 <http://www.coha.dri.edu/web/state_analysis/Colorado/RawahWA_metdesc.html>.

"Razorback Sucker." Rocky Mountain National Park n.d. Web. 13 September 2012 <http://www.nps.gov/romo/naturescience/razorback_sucker.htm>.

Rees, Charlotte Harris. ed. *The Asiatic Fathers of America: Chinese Discovery and Colonization of Ancient America*. Lynchburg, VA: Warwick House, 2006.

___. *Chinese Sailed to America Before Columbus: More Secrets from the Dr. Hendon M. Harris, Jr. Map Collection*. Bloomington, IN: Authorhouse, 2011.

___. *Secret Maps of the Ancient World*. Bloomington, IN: Authorhouse, 2008, 2009.

"Rivers That Flow North" n.d. Web 3 January 2013 http://www.worldatlas.com/aatlas/infopage/riversno.htm.

"Road Trip: San Luis Valley, Colorado" n.d. Web 29 December 2012 <http://www.travel.nationalgeographic.com/travel/road-trips/san-luis-valley-colorado-road-trip/>.

Rocek, Thomas R. and John D. Speth. *The Henderson Site Burials: Glimpses of a Late Prehistoric Population in the Pecos Valley.* Ann Arbor: University of Michigan, 1986.

"Rock Art: Trans Pecos" n.d. Web 21 November 2012 <http://www.texasbeyondhistory.net/trans-p/artistic/index.htm>.

Rogers, Kevin. "Cutthroat Trout" n.d. Web 14 November 2012 <http://www.wildlife.state.co.us/research/aquatic/CutthroatTrout/Pages/CutthroatTrout.aspx#greenback>.

"Ruidosa, Texas" n.d. Web 17 November 2012 <http://www.texasescapes.com/TexasGhostTowns/Ruidosa-Tesas.htm>.

Ruskamp, Jr., John A. *Asiatic Echoes: The Identification of Chinese Pictograms in North American Rock Writing.* Create Space Publishing, 2011, 2013.

___. *The Identification of Chinese Pictograms in North American Rock Writing Addendum 2012.* Create Space Publishing, 2012.

"Salmo Trutta (brown trout)." Nonindigenous Aquatic Species n.d. Web 8 November 2012 <http://www.nas.er.usgs.gov/queries/factsheet.aspx?SpeciesID=931>.

"The San Luis Valley Community Wetlands Strategy" September 2000 Web 19 December 2012 <http://www.wildlife.state.co.us/SiteCollectionDocuments/DOW/LandWater/WetlandsPrograms/stratplan-SLV9-00.pdf>.

"Scenic Drives USA: Los Caminos Antiguos Back Country Byway" n.d. Web 29 December 2012 <http://www.scenicdrivesusa.com/node/67>.

"Scenic Trips to the Geologic Past # 3: Roswell-Ruidoso-Valley of Fires, including trips to Lincoln, Tularosa, and Bottomless Lakes State Park" n.d. Web 17 December 2012 <http://www.geoinfo.nmt.edu/publications/scenictrips/3/>.

Shao, Paul. *The Origin of Ancient American Cultures.* Ames, Iowa: State University Press, 1983.

Sharp, Jay W. "Acoma – A Place to Go Back to" n.d. Web 23 October 2012 <http://www.desertusa.com/mag01/mar/stories/acoma.html>.

Shuler, Ellis W. "Collecting Fossil Elephants at Dallas, Texas." *Field & Laboratory*, Nov. 1934, Vol. III, No. 1, p. 24 (reprinted by permission from *Bulletin of the Texas Archeological and Paleontological Society*, September 1934, Vol. 6).

"Sierra Blanca" n.d. Web 17 December 2012 <http://www.mescaleroapache.com/area/sierra_blanca.htm>.

Simons, Frank S. and William C. Prinz. *Gold*. United States Mineral Resources: U.S. Geological Survey, Professional Paper 820, 1973.

"Site of Ancient Copper Mine: Site of Ancient Copper Mine in Tongling" n.d. Web. 8 October 2012 <http://www.whc.unesco.org/en/tenativelists/5333/>.

Sivinski, Robert A. *Checklist of Vascular Plants in the Sandia and Manzano Mountains of Central New Mexico*. Occasional Papers of the Museum of Southwestern Biology, No. 10, 12 February 2007.

"Ski Apache" n.d. Web 17 December 2012 <http://www.onthesnow.com/new-mexico/ski-apache/ski-resort.html>.

Smith-Savage, Shar and Robert J. Mallouf. *Rock Art of the Chihuahuan Desert Borderlands*. Alpine, TX: Sul Ross State University and Texas Parks and Wildlife Department, 1998.

Snead, James E., Clark L. Erickson, and J. Andrew Darling. *Landscapes of Movement: Trails, Paths, and Roads in Anthropological Perspective*. Philadelphia: University of Pennsylvania Museum of Archaeology and Anthropology, 2006.

Solis, Ruth Shady, Jonathan Haas, and Winifred Creamer. "Dating Caral, a Preceramic Site in the Supe Valley on the Central Coast of Peru." *Science*, Vol. 292, 27 April 2001.

Sorenson, John L. and Carl L. Johannessen. *World Trade and Biological Exchanges Before 1492*. New York: iUniverse, 2004, 2009.

Southerton, Simon G. *Losing a Lost Tribe*. Salt Lake City: Signature Books, 2004.

"Species & Ecosystem Science: Grouse Ecology." Washington Department of Fish and Wildlife Conservation n.d. Web 18 October 2012 <http://www.wdfw.wa.gov/conservation/research/projects/grouse/dusky_sooty/>.

"Species Indication" n.d. Web 14 November 2012 <http://www.wildlife.state.co.us/Fishing/SpeciesID/Pages/FishID.aspx>.

Spencer, Roger, Rob Cross, Peter Lumley. *Plant Names: A Guide to Botanical Nomenclature.* Australia: CSIRO Publishing, 2007.

"State & County QuickFacts – Census Bureau" n.d. Web 11 October 2012 <http://www.quickfacts.census.gov/qfd/index.html>.

Strassberg, Richard E. *A Chinese Bestiary: Strange Creatures from the Guideways Through Mountains and Seas.* Berkeley: University of California Press, 2002.

Stuart, David E. and Rory P. Gauthier. *Prehistoric New Mexico: Background for Survey.* Albuquerque: University of New Mexico Press, 1988.

Studies in Vascular Plants, Mammal Survey, and Data Analysis, Guadalupe Mountains National Park, Texas. Department of Park Administration, Lubbock: Texas Tech University, 1975.

"Sus Scrofa (Feral Pig)." Smithsonian Marine Station at Fort Pierce n.d. Web 29 November 2012 <http://www.sms.si.edu/irlspec/sus_scofa.htm>.

Temple, Robert. *The Genius of China.* Rochester, Vermont: Inner Traditions, 1986, 1998, 2007.

"Texas Geology and Minerals" n.d. Web 17 November 2012 <http://www.utexas.edu/tmm/npl/mineralology/texas_minerals/index.html>.

"This Bites: Venomous Texas Snakes" n.d. Web 20 November 2012 <https://www.dshs.state.tx.us/idcu/health/zoonosis/animal/bites/information/venom/snake/>.

"Traditional Chinese Medicine: An Introduction" n.d. Web 29 January 2013 <http://www.nccam.nih.gov/health/whatiscam/chinesemed.htm>.

"Trans Pecos Mountains and Basins: Artistic Expression" n.d. Web 5 December 2012 <http://www.texasbeyondhistory.net/trans-p/artistic/index.html>.

"Trans-Pecos Mountains and Basins." Vegetational Areas of Texas n.d. Web 20 November 2012 <http://www.uta.edu/biology/meik/classnotes/3310/TexasVegetationLect1/.pdf>.

Bibliography

"Travelers Discover Heritage, Natural Wonders in Texas Mountain Trail Region." *Travel Texas.* n.d. Web 17 November 2012 <http://www.thc.state.tx.us/medallionmag/medalliontravelPDFS/mt_trl_rgn_10.pdf>.

Travel the Historic Turquoise Trail National Scenic Byway: the Perfect Day Trip. Brochure. <http://www.turquoisetrail.org>.

"Treasure with Bill Burrud 1958 – Ben Sublett's Gold Mine" 19 May 2008 Web 21 November 2012 <http://www.youtube.com/watch?v=giAkVKTZ_i0>.

"Tree of Heaven" 7 July 2009 Web 24 October 2012 <http://www.nps.gov/plants/alien/fact/aial1.htm>.

Underwood, Todd. "Frontier Trails of the Old West" n.d. Web 29 December 2012 <http://www.frontiertrails.com/oldwest/oregontrail.htm>.

Upper Arkansas Valley Outdoor Adventure Guide. Salida, CO: Arkansas Valley Publishing Co., 2012.

Vining, Edward Payson. *An Inglorious Columbus.* London: D. Appleton and Company, 1885.

Visitor Guide: Great Sand Dunes National Park. National Park Service, US Department of the Interior.

"Wagon Train and Trail" 2011 Web. 10 October 2012 <http://www.fearfulcrossing.com/Wagontrain&trailHistory.htm>.

Weber, Robert H. "Petroglyphs of the Sierra Blanca." *New Mexico Geological Society Fifteenth Field Conference.* Socorro, New Mexico, 1964.

"Welcome to the City of Albuquerque: Chinese Americans" n.d. Web 4 November 2012 <http://www.cabq.gov/humanrights/public-information-and-education/diversity-booklets/asian-and-pacific-island-heritage-in-new-mexico/chinese-americans>.

"Where's the Trail in Colorado." Continental Divide Trail Society n.d. Web. 11 October 2012 <http://www.cdtsociety.org/colorado.htm>.

"Wild Cane." The Portal to Texas History n.d. Web 15 November 2012 <http://www.texashistory.unt.edu/ark:/67531/metapth88028/>.

"Wildlife Viewing." Rocky Mountain National Park n.d. Web. 18 October 2012 <www.nps.gov/romo/planyourvisit/wildlife_view.htm>.

Witcombe, Christopher L.C.E. "Stonehenge." Art History Resources n.d. Web 23 November 2012 <http://www.arthistoryresources.net/stonehenge/archaeoastronomy.html>.

Wyoming: Historic Trails. US Department of the Interior Bureau of Land Management.

"Wyoming Lakes, River and Water Resources" n.d. Web. 10 September 2012 <http://www.geology.com/lakes-rivers-water/wyoming.shtml>.

"Wyoming Toad: Almost extinct in America's backyard." Amphibian Rescue and Conservation Project 15 October 2012, Web 17 November 2012 <http://www.amphibianrescue.org/tag/bufo-hemiophrys/>.

Xu, Mike. "New Evidence for Pre-Columbian Transpacific Contact between China and Mesoamerica." *Journal of the Washington Academy of Sciences,* Vol. 88 No. 1, Mar 2002.

"Yellowfin Cutthroat Trout/Rocky Mountain Wild" n.d. Web 4 January 2013 <http://www.rockymountainwild.org/species/fish/yellowfin-cutthroat-trout>.

Zhang, Jianping, Houyuan Lu, Naiqin Wu, Xiaoyan Yang, Xianmin Diao. "Phytolith Analysis for Differentiating between Foxtail Millet (Setaria italic) and Green Foxtail (Setaria viridis)" 31 January 2011 Web 19 January 2013 <http://www.plosone.org/article.info%3Adoi%2F10.1371%2Fjournal.pone.0019726>.